S0-DIU-251

FROM THE LIFE

To Harry Howard Bottome the son; George MacDonald Bottome the grandson; and Philip and Nigel Bottome the great-grandsons of Margaret MacDonald Bottome.

by the same author

★

Alfred Adler
The Mortal Storm
Murder in the Bud
Formidable to Tyrants
Heart of a Child
London Pride
Masks and Faces
Within the Cup
Private Worlds

FROM THE LIFE

by

PHYLLIS BOTTOME

FABER AND FABER
24 Russell Square
London

First published in Mcmxliv
by Faber and Faber Limited
24 Russell Square London W.C.1
Second Impression July Mcmxliv
Third Impression January Mcmxlvi
Printed in Great Britain by
Purnell and Sons Limited
Paulton (Somerset) and London

This book is produced in complete conformity
with the authorized economy standards

CONTENTS

INTRODUCTION

In writing these six studies of my friends, I have had three special objects in view. Firstly I wanted to show the direction in which each of these strong characters was going. Secondly I wanted to show the pattern formed in early childhood that was their governing instinct. Thirdly that where there was no conflict—and the goal was directly and unmistakably that of social interest—in the sense used by Adler: 'There is a law that men should love their neighbours as themselves', that these lives proved in every sense of the word highly successful.

Without seeking for either happiness or success, as their immediate goal, but in all three cases that of the good of their neighbours, either intensively and privately as Mrs. James Delano Roosevelt did, or openly and publicly as Adler and my grandmother Margaret Bottome sought to do, they all three obtained both success and happiness.

They were 'whole human beings'. Body, mind and spirit were vigorous, and when attacked re-acted vigorously. They had no nervous breakdowns, no mysterious or long illnesses, no spectacular sins; and each had a rapid and painless death; one upon the threshold of, and two in advanced old age. The bargain between them and life was fairly struck and maintained. They loved life; and life mysteriously repaid them for their love.

Each of the other three friends, as unmistakably followed his special aim, according to his life pattern; but in each of them there was a conflict. They had not got what the painters of to-day call 'the simple approach'. Yet each of them has made a fine contribution to the world and is therefore apposite and open to our study. None of them was an insincere or niggardly giver. The lives of three of them are not yet finished; but they have won so large a measure of success already by their life pattern that it seemed to me not impertinent in the old sense of the word, to trace what their pattern was—and where the knot of conflict arose.

In using my personal friendships with them as a vehicle for these studies I run a certain risk—the risk of their resentment or disapproval; and perhaps that of the public as well, but I run the risk with my eyes open, believing that in the present day we need as never before to study the processes of man's spirit; and that we cannot do better than to take for such a study those spirits who have made, or who are still making, a definite contribution to the times in which they live.

I have known other great people less well than these special six, and still more, other people who were not 'great' in the world's eyes, even better; but the friendships I had with these six particular persons were sincere, and on my part, lively affections, so that I had both incentive and occasion to see how they made their lives; and I feel that my choice of them may have been justified.

I took on purpose individuals of both sexes, because I believe that sex need play a very small part in the shaping of our destinies; and yet that the part it does play has a singular and necessary importance. None of these men was more great because he was a man; and neither of these women less great because she was a woman; but in each the special quality of their greatness was influenced by their sex. You could not put them in each other's places with impunity.

I give the Adler study first, because it was from Adler that I learned Individual Psychology.

I had, as a novelist, always made psychology my life work, but it was not until I met Adler that I learned there was a law as definite as the law of gravity, upon which all human conduct is based; that a man makes himself out of his own acknowledged or more often unacknowledged goal; and it is therefore of desperate importance to us all to learn to choose a right goal; as well as how to unmask our childhood patterns, in order that if we disapprove of their results, we may change our goal to one better suited to our ideals.

It is also perhaps not wholly by chance that of these six friendships chosen at random over a space of many years, two should be with Americans, three with my own countrymen and that the one with an Austrian, the most important of them all, intellectually speaking, should have been with a Jew, since I believe there are no natural barriers between sexes, races or nations, and that any hope for future peace and improvement upon this 'poor earth's crust' largely depends upon our becoming universally minded.

PHYLLIS BOTTOME

I

ALFRED ADLER

'How I should hate to have that man talk to me,' a vivacious lady remarked with a shiver at an Oxford Honour tea, given for Alfred Adler, the great Viennese psychologist; 'He looks as if he could see to the bottom of my soul!' 'No,' one of his students, who had overheard her, ventured to remark, 'the curious thing is you would *not* hate it! It is quite true that Adler would see into the bottom of your soul but he would not condemn you for anything he saw there. He would merely, if you came to him as a student, show you what was really there; and leave it to you to do whatever you wished to do about it.'

Adler was not, in the accepted sense of the word, a teacher at all. He was a creative artist, bent only—as all true artists are—upon understanding the meaning of fact. Nor had he any awe-inspiring quality about him; no-one ever had a more antiseptic absence of mesmeric power. He was—to his students and patients alike—what an expert cracksman is to his fellow burglars with less professional skill. Adler knew how to open the most secret and complicated safes of the mind; and there he sat twiddling away with his burglar's tools and his tremendous wits, until he discovered the exact combination that would swing back the fast closed doors.

First and last he was a workman; he made no sacerdotal claims; and this was the reason of the deep malice roused by him, in certain types of less straightforward psychiatrists. Adler had no interest in money, nor was he out to control his patients; on the contrary he wished to set them free from the adverse control of their own or other people's misdirected love of power, If a patient really wanted to be set free from his difficulties Adler would show him how to release himself.

'A patient', Adler said, 'is like a person in a dark room—he complains to me that he cannot get out. I switch on the light and point to the door handle. If he still says he cannot get out—I know that he does not want to!'

To look at, Adler belonged to what is known as the Pyknic type. He was short, solid, broad-shouldered and highly vigorous. As a young man he had been considered good-looking, and he had always a singularly attractive smile; but in later life, a superficial impression of him was of an agreeable ugliness, but his mouth was shaped beautifully with an optimistic humorous curve upwards; and his hooded deep-set eyes at times were singularly humorous. He had a broad, thinker's forehead; and a very effortless manner. He never drew attention to himself by any physical restlessness. Indeed Adler was usually the last person rather than the first that you would think of in a group, as a remarkable person.

He loved paradox; and his life was largely built up out of paradoxes. He was a philosopher who was known as the most brilliant practising psychiatrist of his day. He was a great psychologist distrusted by many of his medical colleagues because of the weight of his philosophy; and even more distrusted by philosophers because of the common-sense simplicity of his sayings. He was a great speaker and a bad writer, a moralist without a dogmatic belief in any religion. He was a scientist who believed that man is a spirit and therefore responsible for his every act. '*Tout comprendre c'est tout pardonner*' Adler would say 'is quite as true the other way round, *Tout comprendre ce n'est rien pardonner*.'

He was at once the easiest man to know—and the most difficult; the frankest and the most subtle; the most conciliatory and the most ruthless. As a colleague he was a model of generosity, accuracy and whole-hearted integrity; but woe betide that colleague who dared to presume upon his generosity or who was himself guilty of inaccuracy, or who failed in common honesty. For his patients' mistakes, Adler had endless patience, but he never accepted for a fellow-worker any man whom he distrusted. He had a fiery temper, and the patience of an angel. He was a most highly sensitive human being yet he could and did endure, with unruffled equanimity 'the slings and arrows of outrageous fortune'. In spite of losing all his savings during the inflation, his country, and the daily companionship of his dearest friends upon whom his work in Vienna had been built, he remained an unconquerable optimist.

As a scientist Adler never allowed himself to stir beyond the zone of concrete fact. Yet he was the world's best guesser and took every advantage of this great facility.

It was the habit in Vienna of many of the greatest doctors, to call Adler in for consultation to throw light upon a dubious diagnosis. 'Why is it', one of these physicians once asked him, 'that you, who are not an expert in this disease should be able to distinguish it—behind such masking symptoms, while I, who am an expert, have failed?' 'Perhaps', Adler replied, 'it is because I always remember that there is a patient behind every illness.' To one of his own students, a fellow doctor, Adler said, 'You would find it useful, when called in to a new case, always to ask yourself—what does this man want to blow up by this illness?'

One of his most intimate and discerning friends said of him, referring to his sensitiveness to praise or blame, 'Adler had to have a warm bath.' This was more true of him in his earlier years before he had set out to conquer his vanity. He was always pursued by women trying to corner the lavish sea of his affections, but he was never seriously trapped, content as he was to be charmed, since his own serious affections always rested on confidence and reliability. Whenever he found reality in another human being he remained constant. For many years his relationship with his wife was the only unsatisfactory relationship he had; but this was not primarily due to his giving her grounds for jealousy—but rather the great difference in their characters and up-bringing. Raissa was a fervent Russian Leftist, transparently honest—and at any moment only too anxious to assert her fiery principles; whereas Adler was always plastic and rusé and seldom pushed an argument. His 'tenderness' stood in the way of all dogmatic unfriendliness.

Adler minimized every disagreeable element in human intercourse—whereas Raissa swept ahead with her cast-iron convictions, whether they gave pain or pleasure. She was always jealous of her husband's hold over their children.

As a father his life-long friends have said 'Adler was perfect', but perhaps that very perfection grated upon the mother who had had to bear far the greater burden of the children's care in their young years.

Where Adler, all his life, never failed was in helping anyone who needed help. Giving was the whole point of his psychology; and he was always faithful to it. When a friend asked him for a few words to remember and live up to—during a long parting, he said with an unforgettable eagerness: 'Give! You cannot give too much! Give all! All is not enough!'

Adler's character developed greatly in early middle life, when most men's development ceases. The War of 1914 seemed to open up all the channels of his being into fresh activity. He became more and more dependable, more loving, less vain, less explosive, using his ambition to spread his work and ideas rather than to make any personal success or claim.

Perhaps the most vivid and unmistakable of his many gifts was his radiant common sense. He would fully have agreed with the Greek saying, 'It is a disease of the soul to be in love with impossible things'; although he would have thought it equally a disease to set any boundaries to an idea. 'Everything may also be different,' he was fond of saying, 'even what I say to you now may be different.'

'You should not only ask yourself—"What does a bacillus do to a body," he once remarked to a young research worker, 'it is equally important to know what does a body do to a bacillus.'

His sharp cleavage from Freud and even more the length of time before he summoned up the courage to make this cleavage, made an ineffaceable impression upon him. Never afterwards would he overlook the slightest contradiction between Individual Psychology and other theories. 'What are we but midwives', he told a friend, 'helping to bring this child Truth into the world—and there is one thing that makes me mad—when anyone tries to sabotage this child's birth.

His eclectic colleagues deeply resented his refusal to mix his Psychology with theirs, but it was not as many of them thought, because he took a narrow and arrogant approach to the broad field of modern Psychology, but because he believed Individual Psychology to be *not* a mere intellectual theory but rather an attitude towards life itself, without which the mind is not free to choose which path to follow. He never underestimated the great work done by fellow psychologists of other Schools but it would have been as useless to expect Adler to 'mix' his psychology with theirs as to ask St. Paul to share Christianity with the prophets of Baal. 'You cannot divide the Individual,' Adler asserted, 'Man is a whole human being.' Nevertheless it is untrue to say that Adler underestimated the effect upon the individual of heredity, environment, glands and drives; he simply believed that they could be used by the patient in order to escape the full responsibility of normal life. 'Neurosis is an escape from responsibility,' he always taught, or as he sometimes preferred to put it, 'Neurosis is an exploitation of shock.'

Adler set the psychology of use (Gebrauch) in opposition to the psychology of possession (Besitz). How does a man *use* what qualities he has, rather than what qualities *has* he, would have been Adler's first question. He did not deny, as he was often accused of denying—causality, but he believed that heredity, environment and drives act in a teleological rather than in a causal manner.

To Adler, the acid test of a human being was did he perform, however imperfectly, his three main life tasks—work—love—social contacts. Any failure to adjust or effort to escape these three life tasks was to Adler the sign of potential neurosis, or potential delinquency. Any complete refusal to accept *all* these pointed to a probable psychosis.

'A good Individual Psychologist', Adler told one of his patients, 'never lets his wishes master him. He finds out why he has them, and deals with them at their source.' Nor was it ever easy to tell what Adler's own wishes were. He never made a gesture or a sound that might compel attention. Those who met him, took what they wanted from him; and when they wanted, went away. Adler neither hurried them nor held them. 'Shall we come to see you off?' one of his friends asked, before his final leave-taking from Vienna. 'As *you* please,' Adler replied. 'We really want to know if you *like* being seen off!' replied his friend. 'Well,' he said with his usual deep twinkle, 'then I will tell you. I always like to see you—but if you come and see me off when I am going on a long distance journey—then I shall whine!'

Although he rarely showed them, Adler had strong likes and dislikes. He loved music; the drama; cinemas; mountain-walks and swimming. He disliked social small-talk, large entertainments; driving in motors; long railway journeys or eating chicken. Still I have known him do all these things as if he liked them, because he liked much better to have everyone round him pleased than to be pleased himself.

No-one was ever easier to find than Adler, whether he lived with his family in a large flat in old Vienna—or worked for his new country—America—alone in a modest room in a hotel. Nothing was aloof, high-brow, or separate about him. It was as difficult to pigeon-hole any of his qualities as to pigeon-hole the Atlantic Ocean. Adler was any man's and every man's friend. Small, stout, robust, active; abstemious; unrigid; full of the love of living—his twinkling eyes like the eyes of a Paris gamin—his great brow, the brow of a sage—he would sit on the edge of his chair—his feet swinging, as if only a joke could hold him there. 'My science', he wrote to one of his patients, 'has always included gaiety!'

Those who spoke most bitterly of his theories, if they were brought into personal contact with him could not avoid loving him. Nor were they aware that this spontaneous affection gave away their own position, for Adler was the living witness to the truth of his theories—his words had become flesh. This bed-rock sincerity however was by no means always pleasing—people who expected to be charmed, or who relied mainly upon their own charms, were startlingly disappointed in Adler's company. He was as bare of all superfluous foliage as a tree in winter.

He never let himself, or anyone else, off the safe rigidity of fact.

Two of his early memories give the key to the lines of his future work.

As a boy of four, his father took him out for a daily walk, and often stopped to say earnestly; 'Alfred—never believe anything anyone tells you!'

Earlier still Adler remembered being stood on a table to sing a song with this refrain; 'Why did the woman cry at the death of her little hen, when she threw flower-pots at her husband?'

Even at the earliest age, Adler had begun to ask himself: 'Is this feeling real?' His scepticism, in spite of his love for his fellow-men—perhaps because of it—made Adler foolproof.

Compassion and incredulity are strange, but valuable, bedfellows; and it would have been difficult to say which quality was the stronger in Alfred Adler—the pity that made him unhappy if a single ugly baby had an undetected pain; or the impervious scepticism that rose in him like a wall against any fake appeals for his sympathy.

When he could give his confidence he gave it unreservedly. At times his friends thought that Adler put confidence in worthless human beings—but in the long run it generally turned out that either these human beings were—after all—not wholly worthless, and had risen to meet his trust—or that Adler had put limits to his confidence that safe-guarded others.

No-one was less like the standardized saint of religious history than Alfred Adler. He had all the true Viennese love of gaiety and unrigid living. To plan—to tie himself down in any way—was abhorrent to him. A definite date or a fixed duty, imposed a limit upon an elastic future—and his optimism—filled with larger possibilities—always shrank from accepting such limitations.

Could we not wait a little while—' he would beg, when an engagement was being thrust upon him, 'and see what happens later?'

Nevertheless consideration for others was the first law of his life, so that he kept all necessary appointments, with absolute punctuality; paid his bills promptly and could be reckoned on to meet all the usual human obligations.

No-one had to put away, or remember anything for Alfred Adler. He paid as he went, and always resented being put under any obligation. The most he would say to those who insisted upon any offering that furthered his work, was 'Then if you *wish* to co-operate, you may!' but his gratitude was deep for such co-operation; or for any other. 'When a child is being beaten somewhere in China,' Adler once said, 'then we are to blame, for that shows we have not worked hard enough. When there are people anywhere who are anti-social and are not fellow-workers, then we are jointly responsible, because we understand how easily mistakes arise in childhood that distort the world for the child and prevent him from bringing himself into line with other persons. Only when we have done all that we can to co-operate in the development of life; and in working for the welfare of the whole—then only have we done our duty.'

Adler loved an open future as the captain of a ship loves a broad sea way; so that he never found time for merely social interests or invitations.

Adler talked to find out, or to give; but not for any other purpose; and he was the world's best listener.

At first new friends found these long indefinite pauses in general conversation rather perturbing, but Adler's silences were always benevolent and could end in a happy flash of wit, if either of the two openings to his enormous nature were genuinely approached. Tap his generosity—or show him a fact in a new light—and his response—with all his wisdom behind it—was instantaneous.

His new friends soon grew aware of his readiness to give or take facts, and his still greater readiness to meet a human need. It was the pleased, or anxious exposure of vanity, that won no response from Adler; any effort to attract attention through any form of boasting, however skilled or inverted into apparent modesty, was as empty to him as the travelling wind. It blew over him without leaving a trace behind it.

When fellow psychologists complained of the simplicity of his teaching Adler would say, 'I could easily make my psychology difficult; but I preferred to spend forty years in making it simple. I could make it simpler still. I could say 'all neurosis is vanity', but perhaps this also would not be understood!'

He believed that social interest, or as he preferred to call it 'love thy neighbour' could be scientifically instilled into every human being; and he believed without this training in social interest, mankind was doomed to a long period of self-inflicted torture.

'We miss the point of that great story of Cain and Abel,' he once said to a friend, 'for either man *is* his brother's keeper—or he is Cain—and Cain was a murderer. If we do not say 'Yes, I *am* my brother's keeper! we are in Cain's predicament!'

Adler believed that a child should be trained from birth as an equal member of his family, and then prepared through a gradually expanding circle of co-operation, to become a member of the human family.

When Adler spoke of 'equality' he always meant equal to the demands of life.

Man's equality was not to be for his own good alone—though it included his own good—but for the wider good of the human family. He wanted to make each child equal to life itself—then the question of whether he was equal or not to his brother, could hardly seem to him to be of importance.

In his last—and by far the most important of his books *Social Interest; a challenge to Mankind* the house of Individual Psychology is fully built and closed—the scientific steps and proofs of Adler's psychology are handled in this book—with a closeness and authority that finally expresses the man and his work.

Adler saw—as no-one else except the Founder of Christianity

has ever seen—how to handle the human being as a 'whole' and therefore how to get the last ounce out of him. He saw that the full capacities of man cannot be developed by the education of to-day, since it 'picks out parts' and tends to separate a human being from the interests of others.

A child, Adler points out, must be trained from the beginning to face the three main tasks of life—social interest: work: love and marriage—in a spirit of co-operation.

It is only as 'members one of another' that man can become peaceful, liberty loving and self-reliant; if not educated in this way, he becomes a mere isolated atom, led astray by self-interest, tortured by insecurity into a purely artificial love of money, drugged with unmeaning pleasures, and fated by the over-stimulation of a competitive training to eat up, or be eaten up, by his fellow-man.

'If a man has social interest,' Adler often said, 'he will always have courage enough for what he has to face, and if he has not got social interest—there will always come a point where his courage will break down.'

In order to produce this fully socialized and courageous human being, Adler wanted to have all teachers trained in how to distinguish the two menaced types of children, who are deficient in social interest and therefore a danger to their community; the passive frightened child who meets the demands of his environment with a 'yes-but' and who, if his social interest is not developed, will inevitably become neurotic; and the equally menacing child who has an unusual amount of activity but shows *no* interest in others—and who if he does not change may develop in later life into a criminal. 'How can you tell when a child is neurotic?' people often asked him. 'When he gives trouble' Adler would reply.

To train all teachers is more practicable, Adler urged, and a shorter solution than to try to train all parents.

Therefore Adler's later life was devoted mainly to the training of teachers; although doctors, clergy, welfare workers of every description, as well as enlightened parents and all those interested in understanding human nature, can find their profit in studying Individual Psychology.

Adler believed that the danger of present-day education was its instilling of vanity into the life-plan of the child. Each child is taught to value personal prestige and victory over other children rather than the work itself; and he is not taught the service he could give to his community by understanding and doing his work well.

Adler gave three common-sense reasons for avoiding prestige training.

1. A Prestige-thinker divides the strength of both his drive and his aim—he is out for personal victory as well as out for understanding his subject; he is like a man who tries to chase two rabbits simultaneously—he loses both.

2. Prestige-thinking flurries the thinker; and adds to the difficulty of his task, the fear of not pleasing an audience. This is the cause of stage fright—like a centipede in a panic—the Prestige-thinker does not know which leg to start with!

3. Prestige-thinking makes enemies of other people, for they feel it a menace to their own powers—therefore the prestige-thinker not only adds to his own tensions—but he robs himself of the sympathy of the audience which he is seeking; and if Prestige is his aim throughout his life, he will always divide his powers and lose the support of his fellow-men.

Adler believed that all children except the physically feeble-minded could be trained to successful living, if this false stimulation to vanity were replaced by the aim of social interest. They would not then be depending on extraordinary and often terrifying efforts, gifts or chances, but on their own normal working powers.

He also believed that to aim at the service of the community rather than at personal success, infinitely enlarged the scale of human happiness and released unknown stores of courage and creative powers.

Adler spent more than forty years in training teachers to release children threatened by neurosis or delinquency. Thirty-two national schools in Vienna were the main field of Adler's work between the years 1919–1934. The result was the almost complete wiping out of delinquency and neurosis in these schools. The Nazis put an end to his great experiment, but teachers trained in Individual Psychology by Adler never changed in their approach to the child—and such teachers still exist in the schools of Vienna and may one day be released with the store of their knowledge still intact to enrich the world.

Adler's outer and inner life were interchangeable, and both were bound up in his work. He had always had many specialized interests. As a University student his best subjects were anatomy and internal drives. Later he concerned himself specially with eye troubles. To use one of the terms of Individual Psychology, 'the sphere of the visible', had a special attraction for him. As a student and until his marriage, Adler was a great reader; and read with a retentiveness and accuracy that never failed him. He read for 'use' but what he used, he explored to the uttermost. 'He was a good if not a profound scholar', Fortmüller says of him, 'you might even say he *was* a profound scholar—where he was most interested.' But if Adler learned to *see*, even more thoroughly he learned to *hear*. The thing unspoken or kept secret—the harmony or discord in the note of the soul—were never long hidden from him.

After his lectures—when sometimes for an hour or two at a time—he would answer any questions that his audience put to him, it was noticeable how satisfied the questioners always seemed to be with Adler's answers; as if Adler had put out the feelers of his mind, to reach a hidden need. One had the feeling that if each person in the hall had asked the same question, Adler would have given to each, a different answer; and that to each of the questioners his own answer would have seemed to be the truth.

All men owe much to their upbringing; and as Adler believed to the family constellation. He himself was the second son of a large family; and his father's favourite while his elder brother was the mother's favourite, and throughout life Adler's hidden or open rival. 'He was a good man,' Adler once said when describing their relationship, 'though all his life a trouble to me—as I believe I was to him.'

Adler was born on the 7th of February 1870 in Penzing, a suburb of Vienna. One of his friends wrote of him: 'All his life he was proud of his youth spent among the despised workers of these mean streets, and it was there he learned respect for courage and comradeship.' Adler's father was a fairly successful corn dealer, an eccentric, attractive, vain man, who was able to give his eldest children the best education Vienna could provide, and who saw them both on their way to successful careers before failure came upon him. Adler married early a Russian student, whom he adventurously followed to her own country, to carry her off. Raissa had as much character as he had and as much courage. Perhaps her love for Adler was the main pre-occupation of her difficult life. She fought all its problems to a finish, and the courage of both survived the long battle of their independent wills. The last few years of their married life were as nearly perfect as is given to human beings to know 'upon this poor earth's crust'.

Adler had from the first a large and increasing practice, and worked from morning till night. His first step out of the poor working district in which he lived, was a little book on the hygienic conditions of the tailoring trade. This little book —which was read outside his own city—made a great and much needed change in a sweated trade. It frightened the employers and the Public at large by its exposure of the danger from infection, owing to the shockingly low standard of living under which the tailoring trade was carried on. Like all Adler's future writing—this book was more of a deed than a word.

His next step, was his almost reluctant agreement to join Freud's brilliant circle, at Freud's own earnest suggestion. The 'productive antagonism' that followed during the next decade of Adler's life, was a curious study in human relationships. Freud and Adler were devoted friends; Adler was Freud's physician and his deeply trusted colleague—Freud was to Adler, a great and fruitful introduction into a world, upon whose threshold he was already standing. But the eyes of the two men looking into this world, saw in each case a different vision. In 1907 Adler produced *The Study of Organ Inferiority and its Psychic Compensation* and this has always remained a text book in the medical profession. This study of Adler's however was off the track of Freud's mind and he took no interest in it.

The friendship and co-operation between them still continued for a few years more but the rift between them was already visible to their colleagues; and ever widening. As long as Freud's theories followed the critical 'un-masking' so dear to both great thinkers they could work together; but as Freud more and more stressed what Adler called his 'sex-mythology' and refused to expose it to the old relentless method of his youth, Adler drew further and further away from him. At last the tug-of-war finished in an explosion. Adler—to Freud's great regret—left his circle with nine of its foremost thinkers, mainly the young writers with Leftist politics, while Freud remained with his band of faithful psychiatrists, who never ceased to treat Adler as the worst, as he was certainly the most formidable, of their enemies. It was not perhaps surprising that these experts remained with Freud, for he provided them with well-paid foreign patients; and a long and complicated system of analysis which brought them not only good financial results, but also ministered to their power instincts, for it was quite impossible for the public to follow their recondite terms or to take over their complicated cures for themselves.

Adler had only four years to start, with his fellow thinkers, the building up of his School of Individual Psychology, before the war struck Vienna, and carried him off to work for the Forces.

It was late in 1916 before he returned to the starving pallid spectre of his beloved Vienna. 'What have you to give us?' his old cronies demanded, on his first entrance to his old café. 'I think what the world needs most is *Gemeinschaftsgefühl*,' the new Adler answered thoughtfully. 'Who has ever heard of *Gemeinschaftsgefühl*, it is not a word used in philosophy?' groaned the brilliant Alexander Neuner.

The proud intellectuals and Nietzsche's will-to-power men now got up and left the café, never to return; but Neuner lingered. 'I always knew', he said later, 'that when Adler said anything, it could somehow or other be *done*, so I waited to see how; and I am glad that I waited.'

Adler explained that he had discovered a law by which to develop scientifically the diseased and despairing heart of man. Man must—and therefore he *could*—learn to release his cramped and shackled powers, through loving his neighbour as himself. This law, Adler explained, could be made the foundation of education in the life of every human being.

Naturally the doctors did not wish to take any part in such 'missionary talk'. Some of them watched with bitter envy Adler's enormous success in therapeutic psychiatry. 'It was a great experience', one colleague wrote, 'to watch with humility how the patient was transformed into a human being under Adler's guiding hand. Raging maniacs became quiet while he spoke to them, fascinated by the fact that they had met a man who understood them, and appealed to the latent human being still within them. We were permitted to witness with him how from behind the symptoms, illness, and mental torment there gradually emerged a human being, who for the first time learned from Adler to see himself, recognize his errors and gain courage to construct another and better life—a life that would make its true worth real. . . . Adler himself was so ready to get into touch with people, and so capable of doing it that even the most unwilling and refractory of his patients was unable to elude him. All that was dark and unintelligible vanished before Adler's personality with its sympathy into the patient's inmost being. The most complicated symptoms were dissolved, and on the background of the neurosis, there stood out crystal-clear the personality of the individual who had created it.'

But such successes though they gained Adler a solid reputation among fellow psychiatrists, and brought him innumerable private patients, roused considerable jealousy among some of his colleagues. The stick most used by these psychiatrists as a weapon against Adler's theories was always his 'short treatments' or his 'missionary spirit'. It has never been a popular thing among doctors that patients should treat themselves; and it was this that Adler demanded of all his students.

It is difficult to describe the effect of Adler as a personal friend, since his friendship always seemed to be a universal emanation radiating good-will and courage—rather than a private or personal affection. But he certainly had preferences and he certainly chose companions; although they were not always the ones that he might have been expected to choose. He loved giving his friends presents, and finding out any ways in which he could serve their wishes and it was quite extraordinary how often in absence he managed to send them his short but constant letters.

Perhaps what he loved most in his friends was what he could set free in them, and what he respected most in his chosen comrades was their human quality. 'There is such a great danger', he remarked wistfully to one of his friends, 'in being so often in the right—could you not vary this a little?'

If it was difficult to tell what kind of a feeling his friends roused in Adler, it was much more easy to understand the emotion he roused in them. 'What should you feel', his daughter Ali asked a friend just after Adler's death, 'if we could have my father back with us again?' 'Secure' this friend answered. His daughter thought for a moment, then she said, 'I shouldn't—I should feel enriched.'

To all who needed him most Adler gave a feeling of bottomless confidence. He was a cook who would never poison you—not if all the world were turned into Borgias.

To those who less needed help, as his daughter had discovered, he added to the happiness his companionship brought them, the sense of larger possibilities in life. He was by no means a great talker. Often he would sit the whole evening in a café with a group of his friends and hardly open his mouth; but if he were there it would be a happier—more tolerant group. Sometimes Adler talked brilliantly, but seldom at length, an apposite joke, a flash of wit—a sudden piercing thought would fall unforgettably into their listening hearts. If he had an opinion or a fact that could fit well into a discussion, he liked to fit it in—as if the group round him were working together with him on a picture-puzzle and he had just happened on the right piece; but he never went off into a monologue, or separated himself in any way from the lesser minds that formed his company. He was a perfect host because he always saw that each guest had a chance to make his own particular contribution; and he was an equally good guest—which is a rare quality in a man who makes an ideal host—since he was ready to enjoy any pleasure his friends prepared for him.

Nevertheless Adler was often a challenge to his company for to expect the truth from another human being and relentlessly to give it to him, is always a challenge.

There were certain types of conversation for which Adler always had an aversion. He never liked to listen to personal complaints, and he disliked any topic that was unnecessarily disagreeable. Not that he would object or shrink from any sharpness of speech that cleared up a wrong—the sharper the better; but to give pain to another person by talking about things that might offend or discourage him was anathema to Adler. He never allowed a person to be baited or discouraged in his presence without instantly intervening in no uncertain manner. In public Adler was a great Fighter; and he made many enemies; but he chose them well. They were not people anyone of judgment would have cared for as friends.

'My enemies have always blessed me', Adler remarked three days before his death. 'It is true that when they do not resent my ideas they may often run off with them, and call them their own; but they will spread them the more readily on that account! I believe that in my life-time, I have made some useful discoveries and that therefore they will be of lasting service to mankind; and this makes me happy.'

It is not too much to claim for Adler that if it had not been for the Dictatorships, he would have developed throughout Europe, a psychological education that might have changed, and would certainly have quickened, the whole outlook of mankind.

Just as Hitler conceived and executed—with the help of

the Rich and Powerful in the German Nation—an education of the young towards hate; so Adler, twenty years before Hitler came into power, thought out and perfected a system of education to teach young people how to love and respect their neighbours. Upon Adler's system of child culture the good citizenship of a future world depended; but unlike Hitler, he won no rich and powerful citizens to back his discoveries.

'If thine eye be single,' the Bible tells us 'thy body shall be full of light.'

Hitler, who was a boy at the time of Adler's control of the Viennese Schools, may well have learned the teleological significance of the singleness of aim from Individual Psychology, but while Adler taught the teachers to train their children towards Light, Hitler, twenty years later, taught the whole of Germany to train their young towards darkness.

'There is a Law', Adler was never tired of saying, 'that man should love his neighbour as himself—in a few hundred years it should be as natural to mankind as breathing or the upright gait; but if he does not learn it—he must perish.'

It was for the sake of this law that Adler fought all his later battles and lost some of the greatest and most brilliant of his adherents. Adler always insisted upon keeping Individual Psychology simple enough for the poorest to understand it. He got rid one after the other, of all careerists whose secret aim was to use what was meant for mankind, in order to line their own pockets.

A weapon often used to deprive him of support, or of the honour due to his rising reputation among world authorities outside his own city, was that Adler involved himself in Politics. Politics in Austria at the moment were trying to undermine the freedom of the individual and tampering with personal responsibility. This was unendurable to Adler, since he believed that to tamper with the personal responsibility of any human being was to destroy humanity at its source.

So deeply did Adler feel the vital importance of the individual conscience that he did an almost unprecedented thing for a Jew and a Viennese. He publicly joined the small Protestant Sect in Austria. This at one stroke deprived him of the support of the Jewish people—and of the Catholics. He spoke once for the Soldiers' and Sailors' Council under the Social Democratic Government which further damned him: though he spoke only to explain to them the system of Individual Psychology. He horrified his now middle-aged and highly respectable colleagues by sitting in soup kitchens with tramps and the poorest of the working people of Vienna. He did this because after the war he had to build up his practice again, with a growing family whom he wanted to educate in the best way possible; and it must also be admitted that Adler always preferred tramps to pedants. Still Adler had a great respect for his own profession, and was a faithful scientist, nor did he ever criticize his colleagues. It was his life that was a silent reproach to some of them; and a reproach that the more commercially-minded and power-loving never forgave.

One of his life-long friends said of this period, 'It was a different Adler that grew out of those war years. A man more earnest, more grave, more strong. He had not lost his sense of humour or his charm, but he had no time for social life—he became wholly absorbed in his work. He gave everything he had to his patients and to friends; only we who worked with him realized what a world of strength and knowledge he had to give.'

Adler knew that he ran a race against time, for he well saw that the Europe he loved was swiftly moving in the wrong direction.

'What miracles you have accomplished,' one of his friends said to him one day. 'People now come from all over the world to study your child clinics; and listen to your lectures!'

'Ah! But the world moves so slowly!' Adler said with unusual sadness, 'and we have so little time!'

He saw the small cloud no bigger than a man's hand, clearer than anyone else, and knew that it would one day soon blacken out Europe. As early as 1927 he decided to try out the possibilities of the New World. He set out over the sea, at sixty, with no knowledge of the English language to make a new career for himself in a strange land. Because of his democratic leanings, he had no backing from the University of Vienna, though America was quick to realize his real standing and soon made a chair of Psychology for him at the Long Island College of Medicine, which he held for seven years with increasing success and understanding, till his death in 1937.

Adler only had these seven years in which to found his new science in Anglo-Saxon countries—a science that had the basic truth of all religions for its goal.

He died in full career, at the height of his powers, with his hopes unaccomplished, and the growing cloud of a fresh world war now plain upon the horizon.

'How is your work getting on?' a friend asked him, three days before his sudden death. 'It goes on splendidly!' Adler replied, his face lit up with joy, 'You see, I have such marvellous friends!'

He was fond of saying to impatient and anxious disciples, 'Yes—but we must look at all this in the space of eternity', and the ease with which he met all the terrific pressures and the many tragedies of his life, bore out his fundamental optimism. His life was filled to the brim with work; for years he worked sixteen hours a day without apparent fatigue. He had no serious illnesses, except one three years before his death from which, though grave, he recovered with extraordinary ease and rapidity.

He still saw patients from breakfast to bedtime; with breaks for an occasional lecture. He wrote over a dozen books; as well as countless articles; and largely contributed to the journal of Individual Psychology which he founded, first in Vienna and then re-founded later in Chicago.

The publications which perhaps were of the greatest permanent interest to his medical and psychiatrist colleagues were; *Study of Organ weaknesses and their psychical Compensation*, *Theory and Practice of Individual Psychology* and *The Nervous Constitution*.

Those that should be a part of every teacher's life, were

Social Interest: A Challenge to Mankind and *Understanding Human Nature.*

These two are probably the best translated and easiest to read of all Adler's books. For the general public, *What Life should mean to you,* has the widest appeal. From Adler's note-books, brilliantly edited by Philip Mairet, *Problems of Neurosis* stands out, as interesting to all students of psychology.

Yet in spite of his enormous output both of written and spoken words, Adler always gave the impression of leisure. As his patients or friends saw him, sitting opposite him in his little New York study, Adler might have been a timeless Buddha on a Lotus leaf.

Yet he had very little help in his work, and never possessed a trained secretary. Generally someone serving as a secretary was in his later years attached to him, either a patient in need of money, or of psychological training, and he or she was supposed to keep Adler's appointments and write some of his letters for him; but the helping hand was very seldom the secretary's.

Adler did not possess a car. Sometimes his friends took him to and fro, for his appointments, more often he went alone on street cars or trams.

He was seldom late for an engagement and most business-like and dependable in all his habits; and yet he seemed to have no habits. A man more adjustable to circumstances or quicker to see when and how the best of rules must be broken never existed.

One might say that all his nearest relationships had been chosen with a view to making life as difficult for himself as possible. Yet they were relationships he had chosen; and he made a triumphant success of most of them. His married life was anything but a bed of roses; probably no more challenging and provocative partners ever tried to pull together in double harness. His four children full of talent, independence and originality all adored him. They gave him intense pleasure, and often nerve-racking pain. Yet out of these nettles of Danger, Adler plucked an inner safety as deep and satisfying, as if he had lived in a land of sunshine, where citrons bloom forever. He had friends in every country and every city he ever visited, from bell-boys to Presidents of Universities. But perhaps there were even more bell-boys than Presidents.

His daughter Ali once told me—'Father has never had many influential friends'. But whatever they were, Adler loved them and built out of his friends the deepest joy of his rich life. Perhaps the best of all his friends was life itself. No man has ever enjoyed life more, or understood it better.

2

MAX BEERBOHM

In the bland innocuous world of yesterday, Rapallo was a charming little town for a self-exiled artist to choose as a home.

It was colour-washed in pale pinks and yellows, the smoke of olives and the purple bloom of mountain gorges. Cypresses pin-pointed their fastidious way up the steep slopes behind the little city; while the Mediterranean 'coiled', or uncoiled, its blue 'streams' ever changingly, in front of it.

It was not strange perhaps that Max Beerbohm should have chosen such a favoured spot for his home, only strange that his retirement—at the height of his fame, with all London at his feet—should have become so absolute. His place in London was secure; and he was beautifully befriended, nor had he the favourite motive of those who, like Anna Karenina and Vronsky, had to seek the shelter of the 'small Italian towns' in order to enjoy in quiet seclusion the fruits of illicit love. On the contrary he took with him an equally famous consort who had been the greatest interpreter of Ibsen's heroines on the Anglo-Saxon stage—Florence Kahn. She had consented to become Mrs. Beerbohm; and the obscurity the Beerbohms sought must consequently have had a good deal to say for itself; nevertheless the fact remains that they sought an exile that involved personal isolation.

Perhaps their chief motive was that they had found the world they left only too friendly. As one of Henry James' heroes softly murmurs on his death bed, as an excuse for prematurely fading away from a world that loved him—'too many things—too many people'. But whatever his reasons may have been, what neither of them fully realized was the price an artist has to pay for severing himself—for any great length of time—from his audience. The artist does not necessarily lose his audience, since he can—if he is a writer—entertain them from a distance; but he himself gets lost.

The Villino, where the Beerbohms made their home, was as inconspicuous as possible. A big pink villa, from which it took its name, faced the main gateway, and gave it the protection of its own publicity. A little to the left, hidden by enchanting trees and flowering bushes, the Villino bloomed secretly and brilliantly under the brow of an olive-covered hill, and with a life completely of its own.

The roof, and a small tower room opening out on to it, were alone exposed to the full glories of the sea and the view. From this point of vantage the eye could range along the pearl and coral-pink coast to Sestri Levanti, and across the bay to where the three little acorn-shaped, olive-covered hills waded out from Portofino into the azure sea. A big studio room and a still smaller villino were buried in the garden; a cottage resurrected by Florence Beerbohm from some poor use as a pig sty or abode for roaming goats and chickens, had been turned by the hand of an artist into a dream for visiting angels.

Nothing could have been more enchanting, more surprising, than the amount of space these small buildings managed to cover and conceal. They were secluded even from each other. Every room was a separate and shining work of art, emanating direct from the creative beings who inhabited it. Perhaps neither of the Beerbohms had originally intended to make quite such a definite end to their public lives when they first settled in the Villino. London was always there, they could (and did) from time to time refreshingly go back to it. Their friends visited them frequently and gladly. Yet the wall grew thicker and higher between them and the outer world. Like the Pharaohs of Ancient Egypt—only prematurely—the Beerbohms were buried in a secret place; and their treasures were buried with them.

There were few things that Max Beerbohm liked about the work of much younger writers, yet he was too timeless an artist, as well as too benevolent a human being, not to catch occasionally a gleam of something for which he had a definite value; and to which he could, and did, react with great generosity. Such a letter full of that deep encouragement of a fellow craftsman reached me from him once, in a desolate hour during a serious illness; and it is perhaps not too fanciful to think this unexpected gift beckoned me on towards a renewed desire for life. The letter contained an invitation which could not be immediately accepted. When it was possible, a year later, in 1935, to make a visit to Rapallo, the dreadful end of the Fascist venture was already casting its first long shadows.

Max Beerbohm saw, long before anyone else did, and with dreadful clarity, what awaited the land he loved. He already belonged to something threatened; so did liberty; and if Max Beerbohm loved anything better than privacy, it was liberty. He sat there in his beautiful menaced Paradise waiting for the God he perhaps least cared for—the God of Mars—to drive him out of it.

In this world of increasing rigidity, Max Beerbohm kept his personal freedom of thought elastic, and inviolate. Among the people who visited the villino, those who were German Liberal-minded, or those of Jewish origin, exiled from their native land, must have felt, as they received the exquisite hospitality handed out to them—perhaps even emphasized by the deep unspoken sympathy of their hosts—as if they were enjoying a glimpse of a lost Paradise.

Here, under this roof, minds could reveal themselves unshaken by fanciful restrictions of race or birth—or the more real and implacable distinctions between barbarism and civilized thought. Here—and perhaps only here during those fatal years under the soft Italian skies—stars dared to differ from each other in glory.

There seemed to me in Max Beerbohm's courteous silence about the Régime he hated, and even in his suave admission that it had done some good at the outset, a cold ferocity. There was almost nothing left for him—even in Rapallo—that he could care for. Monstrosities of new buildings broke up the soft line of the lovely coast. Hideous mechanical noises shook and ravaged the quiet countryside. Suffocating dust from death-dealing motor lorries clogged the bright air. Far more dreadful even than these were the barbaric ideas stored up in the minds of the Fascist youth of Italy, trained and equipped for nothing beyond aggression.

All Max Beerbohm had ever asked of the outer world was to leave him alone; and it was not even going to allow him that immunity much longer. I shall never forget the last picture of the rigorous beauty maintained by those two deeply civilized beings, upon the edge of what they both knew to be—doom.

Max Beerbohm never pressed his gifts upon anybody, either as an artist or as a host. There they were. When once the requisite ceremonies had been disposed of, you were welcome to share them, at the price of your wits. Even if you used the best you had, it was easy to go away having overlooked some treasure of taste, some gently dropped pearl of unaggressive wisdom flitting back into the mind afterwards as an unacknowledgeable debt.

Each room and its contents were part of the Beerbohms' welcome; and what the visitor saw was the result of consummate personal taste; austere training; and complete intellectual equipment.

Peace has its battles as well as its victories; but the Beerbohms' guests were offered only the victories.

Their welcome—and I doubt if they would have invited guests whom they did not want to see—was the background of the situation. They did not keep their guests waiting; they stood in an open doorway; and this right to enter, once established, the visit could hardly fail to be—except through some dire failure on the part of the guest himself—a triumphant success.

What struck me most about them on that first meeting was that though they should, by the mere lapse of time, have been old, they were not. Time had, as the air-pilots say, 'taken evasive action', and left the Beerbohms in a region where the weight of its passage had no concern. The region they inhabited was art—the supreme art—of living.

I doubt if this art will ever be offered again, quite as the Beerbohms offered it. They had studied the five senses with a peculiar felicity. Both loved colour; both understood form; and neither of them liked excess or exaggeration. I never ate a finer meal than in that sunny, flower-scented little dining-room, noislessly waited on by a tenderly attentive Italian servant; but just because it was so exquisite, and the wine had the same quality as the sunshine, what it was exactly that we ate escapes the memory. The food simply went with the conversation.

It was April, and the flowers of April, the light and texture of April, bloomed over the whole occasion.

It is often said that artists are not like what they produce; but I do not think this has ever been said of them by other artists. Mrs. Browning knew better when she declared that the 'wine must taste of its own grapes'.

Max Beerbohm was an illustrated edition of his own essays. He talked exactly as he wrote, only there hung upon the words themselves the bloom of his personality. His wit reached his listener without even the trouble of having to turn the printed page, playing upon the conversation, as the April sunshine played upon the yellow tulips, so freely arranged on the table. Barbs would not have been in order. Phrase followed phrase sparkling as the golden wine; and like the wine not too sweet—and with as tonic a flavour.

Max Beerbohm never for an instant stood in the way of anyone else's wit. On the contrary as a host he acted as a stimulant to the wit of others. You never had a feeling that he was turning a phrase, but rather as if he were giving it plenty of room to turn itself, and merely supplying for it the encouragement of light, oxygen and laughter.

On this first occasion, I seem to remember we talked mostly of books—books attached to the special gifts and idiosyncrasies of their authors. I remember quoting to him a certain criticism of Alice Meynell's on Jane Austen's novels: 'They are too little heavenly', the poet had said of the great prose writer. 'But why should she have *been* heavenly?' Max smilingly objected. 'After all—Heaven wasn't her subject.'

He himself was quite prepared to laugh—and to be heavenly—at the same moment. Will any grateful reader ever forget his description of Elysium in 'No. 2 The Pines'? But he wouldn't have laughed at art. Art was to him—Religion. I can well imagine that if a friend of Max Beerbohm had been a moral delinquent, this kindly artist would have looked the other way; and even if he had had stones in his hand at the time, never have dreamed of throwing even the smallest pebble. But he would have thrown any stone he had, and gone out to look for more, at the sight of a dishonest or slovenly piece of writing!

Without being catholic in his taste, Max Beerbohm was extremely anxious to be just, and took infinite pains to understand what any genuine artist meant, even when he most fervently disliked and resented the vehicle of his style.

All he demanded as a critic, and this he demanded to the last drop of his blood, was that an artist's work should match his own conception of what was right. An artist without a conception of what was right, Max Beerbohm would not, I think, have admitted to be an artist.

If he himself preferred the eighteenth century as a medium for style, it was partly because he liked its special control of emotion; and partly because scepticism seemed to him a less doubtful quality than faith. Faith might stack an ace up your sleeve; but scepticism pulled it down. Humbug was what he despised most; but he could not have despised it as much had he not worshipped truth. He never hid his scorn; but his worship he may sometimes have concealed rather too successfully.

Still he would never have been the great dramatic critic that he was, had he wanted in the modern manner, to bagatellize the emotions. He knew they were the stuff of life itself; but he wanted to throw upon them light, rather than heat.

Probably no monosyllabic hard-boiled modern youth shrinks with so passionate a distaste from sentimentality as Max Beerbohm shrinks from it. We have only to read his essay on 'Peter Pan' to realize that those fierce body-thrusts at Barrie sprang from sharp repulsion.

Still 'Max' does not underestimate the part of any great emotion that springs direct from a primary and natural cause. Otherwise he could not have so valued the acting of Sarah Bernhardt or the drama of King Lear.

But there is one curious gap in his appreciation of great dramatic art. He could not bear Duse. She affected him as cats are said to have affected the late Lord Roberts, or as some people shudder at the texture of slugs. He was neither fair about her, nor reasonable, nor kind. Something in the power and passion of this spiritual and tremendous personality lashed him into positive fury. She was simply too much for him, as she was said to have been—in quite another sense—for D'Annunzio.

But Sarah had no such effect upon him. Sarah he loved, understood and enjoyed. He criticized her acting with infinite exactitude but with no faintest shadow of irritation. Perhaps his hatred of Duse was because he could not laugh at her—or indeed with her; since there was no laughter in Duse.

During one of these kind and felicitous hours which we spent under their roof, the Beerbohms, with infinite courtesy, but no doubt some anxiety, permitted me to read them aloud a short story I had written founded upon 'Sarah'. A mere guessed-at, imagined 'Sarah', for my actual eyes had never beheld this great actress. I did not realize at the time how great a generosity this permission really implied, for it was not till later that I discovered that whereas I knew practically nothing about Sarah, my hosts knew practically everything. Nevertheless they managed to make it a very happy occasion. They were both interested in the study I had tried to make of her; and afterwards we discussed for hours the art of the theatre, and its greatest exponents.

I wish I could remember Max Beerbohm's actual words, for I never again heard him speak with quite so much fervour and felicity. He re-fought old battles; he drew out old treasures; he re-created Sarah. How, as an artist, I wished that I had heard him speak *before* and not *after* I had written *The Cup of Alteration.* Every sincere and growing writer must have found him, as a critic, the kindest and clearest of guides.

Any possible strength or gift there is in another person's writing he sees, and like a careful gardener fosters; and, equally like a careful gardener, he prunes as he goes. I once remarked to a successful rose-grower, who had been a great surgeon, 'How is it each single blossom of your roses is so perfect a bloom?' 'Well,' he explained, 'you see, I am a surgeon, I take great care never to wound any more than I can possibly help when I prune.' I do not know if the literary blossoms of Max Beerbohm's tending came out as well as the surgeon's roses, but I think he used the same economy in cutting. 'I hope you will not always write such short sentences,' he once said to me, 'it is as if you couldn't draw a long breath.'

His own sentences have a peculiar charm, because he used the flexibility of the English language to its fullest extent without ever violating the rigour—where there is rigour—of its laws.

He did not only say unexpected things; but he said them in an unexpected way. Every word danced in the careful minuet of his mind with self-created steps, while keeping exact time, nevertheless, to unheard music. Yet youth, modernity, the future of art itself—all were tarred for him at this period of 1935–36 with the same fatal brush. The shadows were too thick upon him.

He felt that the forces behind them were breaking down the private life.

It was Everyman, who was knocking at the door; and it was precisely Everyman whom Max Beerbohm desired to keep out.

Anything communal he revolted from. He understood and pitied, he even respected the resentments of the under-dog. He had none of the top-dogger in his own free spirit; unless indeed the refusal to be responsible for the under-dog may be to participate in this elusive vice. I am sure that he treated everyone less gifted than himself—child, beggar or dog, that he met, with the same considerate courtesy, but he did not consider the wrongs of mankind to be his business. If the world had to have wrongs, let them be righted by some specially busy or emphatic person—such as Mr. Gladstone for instance, Lord Shaftesbury or Annie Besant. Mass production, mass opinion, mass conscience, Max Beerbohm loathed them all.

Intimate, sustained and permanent affections he thoroughly believed in, but all swift indiscriminate contacts—the mixing up of things he thought should be kept indelibly separated—were to him the unpardonable sin. He wanted light and air as much as most people; he wanted truth more than most people wanted it, and was prepared to pay a high price for it; but what he didn't want was too much life.

Even in the ardent years of his successful youth in London he had rather too much of it, or else he would never have retreated into the hushed confinement of Rapallo. Now Life, noisy and exacting, had overtaken him even there; and he hated it—as he had hated Duse. Everything was coming out of its appropriate pigeon-hole and melting into everything else. Hideous houses blocked the soft old crumbling solitudes; the chestnuts were cut down to make room for what he didn't want; the peaceful empty shrines were being hustled into—by goodness knows who—looking for goodness knows what. The Private Life was over; even before Mussolini began to fill the gap with public death.

I once took a child of three into a shop of modern—and as I myself thought, specially charming and artistic—toys. It was his birthday and I told him to take what he liked. He looked all round him with anxious eyes; and burst into tears. 'I couldn't like it!' he cried, rushing in desperation from one toy to the other. 'I couldn't like it!'

Just such an agony of useless choice confronted Max Beerbohm in this modern world. His gorge rose at what he saw before him. It was too much! It was not enough! It was all wrong!

Yet the thing that makes Max Beerbohm's work timeless, his every line significant, is still needed. 'Why do you not write', I pleaded, '*the* memoirs of the nineteenth century? You are the only person who was in it up to the eyes, without being part of it! No-one else could write of it just as you could, with familiarity and objectivity at the same time.' 'Perhaps I could', he said gently, but a little sorrowfully, 'only I don't think I want to!'

It had moved, this nineteenth century, to which he rather reluctantly belonged in point merely of time, in what was for him, the wrong direction. He could not follow it down the slope of the twentieth century, covered as it seemed to him with Gadarene swine, all prancing together towards a fatal precipice. 'To each his need; from each his power.' This might be all very well as a goal for the Poet of to-morrow; but the poet of yesterday sang differently.

The curious thing about this retreat of Max Beerbohm's is that though he was quite prepared—indeed even anxious—to dispense with the life of the day, the Day was not in the least prepared to dispense with him.

The tragedy of the old is generally that what they have to give is no longer wanted; but Max Beerbohm's tragedy was quite another kind—he simply no longer desired to give what the world still wanted. The young loved his soft explosions of humbug; they yearned for more, and still more, of his disinfectant style. They liked everything he had ever written. They wanted to see him; to tell him so; to share with him all their terrible problems; to rush him into their air-born predicaments. Where they made their mistake was that they expected him to like *them*; and in the lump, he didn't. Individually and selectively he enjoyed certain young people; but collectively—and with the objects he suspected them of wanting to collect—he did *not* like them. He didn't want to go in their direction. He thought most of their problems piffle—or if not piffle—appalling. He wanted—as he had always wanted; but now more vehemently than ever—to be left alone.

He had returned to his own country; but it was not a prodigal's return; and he neither deserved nor desired a prodigal's welcome. He did not like fatted calves. He preferred something more carefully thought out; and less fat.

Twice upon the radio he as good as told the British young exactly what he thought of them.

Yet Max Beerbohm must have seen how modern London prized him. When Clemence Dane with admirable skill reset his jewel in prose, *The Happy Hypocrite*, into drama, it was acted by Ivor Novello with a finish and verve which proved this actor as intellectually wide awake as he has always been emotionally attractive—but the best dramatic critic London has ever known was not deluded by the shimmer of that great First Night audience. Both of the Beerbohms felt that the theatre was too large for the smallish audience of permanently enthralled people who might have followed this perfect fantasy throughout the season; spreading its fame over the whole Island; not that the Beerbohms wanted fame but they wanted fitness. The theatre was too large and the audience therefore too indiscriminate. Perhaps there are not so many intelligent people in London as that large theatre could permanently have held. It was an Ivor Novello audience, and since he was acting the chief part could not have been otherwise; and Ivor's audience is not so intelligent as its creator; for them *The Happy Hypocrite* with its flying cupids and lack of coarser appeal was too much to swallow and not enough to eat.

I met the Beerbohms on the evening of the successful first night, after the most enchanting and memorable entertainment had been acclaimed, by a large and enthusiastic audience.

The Beerbohms were generous in their praise of the play and its presentation; but they did not believe in that wildly enthusiastic audience. They suspected the indurability of its texture; and its size meant less than nothing to them.

Their faces wore the expression of the Princess in the fairy tale affronted by the presence of a pea under the nine mattresses. They were nice about the mattresses—they were—the Beerbohms realized for the moment—soft; but they were bitterly aware that the pea would work up; and it did. The audience melted; and the play had to be withdrawn long before the core of intelligent London had had enough of it. Each of the Beerbohms in turn stood unshrinkingly the test of this new British Public; and each gave to the full—the measure of his spirit.

Florence Kahn acted, on the unforgettable night of Ben Greet's dying Shylock, Katharine of Aragon, in the trial scene from *Henry VIII.* It was as if the Queen herself, subtle and proud, honest and implacably legitimate—both as wife and queen—slipped out of history, to confront once more the enigma of Henry's faithless heart.

Neither Henry, nor his time-serving priests, could successfully challenge her sad integrity. Florence Kahn moved, spoke, suffered, before our eyes as the Spanish Queen herself suffered; and even Henry had not dared to kill this queen.

The presentation of their arts finally consummated, silently the Beerbohms retired together, into the private life.

The Public still wanted them to stand as godparents to the child of the future; but they gently waived away any such dubious responsibility.

Yet Max Beerbohm has given his priceless gift to the world of Tomorrow, in spite of himself. There is something in his work that the new world wants; and its yell for it, however discordant the sound may be to his ears, strikes a note that he cannot altogether repudiate. What the claim is, and what he gives towards it, is his fundamental rectitude. The new world wants to be honest; it will not survive if it is not honest; and Max Beerbohm has never written anything but the truth. It is his own truth and only his own; but truth is not private; nor perhaps is art. It is—for us as well as for him—a tragedy that our debt is not on as large a scale as his powers.

Yet there has been no final drop of the curtain upon that meticulous pen. 'Lytton Strachey'—as the Reed lecture for 1943 startlingly and happily reminded us—proves that the mind of the master though silent, is not asleep.

From the first enchanting sentence to the last we have 'Max' at his happiest. I do not say his 'best'. For who is to be the judge—when a man knows how to judge for himself as 'Max' knows—what *is* his private 'best'?

We only know that he has given us what his subject deserved; and would not have got from any other critic. The happiness lies in the subject. We might well have suspected that had 'Max' a favourite disciple it would have been

'Didymus' and Strachey reminded him of Didymus—the deliberate, sensible, fastidious, faithful doubter.

Here was a man younger then himself with a mind exactly to his taste, a timeless, exact, peculiar and imaginative writer.

Lytton Strachey had pleased 'Max' by his looks and perhaps the great Viennese psychologist, Alfred Adler, was not wrong when he insisted a man's mind—since he *is* a 'whole human being'—is interpreted by his person and his gestures. When Max Beerbohm read *Eminent Victorians* he knew that he had found an artist who expressed the man he had liked at sight, on their first meeting.

Perhaps two more complete and indivisible artists had seldom come across each other so successfully in time and space.

How exquisitely in this short essay Max describes his spiritual contemporary. 'Perfect justice is a divine attribute. Lytton Strachey being merely a human being, had it *not*. He had, like the rest of us, imperfect sympathies. Great strength of character, keen practical sense and efficiency, for example, did not cause his heart to glow so much as one might wish they had. They seemed rather to give him a slight chill.' Yet how fully, with what infinite perception 'Max' shows the strength of Strachey's 'Portrait' on the larger scale of 'Queen Victoria'!

Perhaps all great artists need the careful interpretation of one as great or greater than themselves, certainly until I read Max Beerbohm's essay on Strachey I may have known what I liked in him—but how seldom *why* I liked it! 'Max' has now taught us why. He has taught us too his subject's limitations. Strachey had *not* the surgeon's deep-cutting merciful cruelty at his most vital and vigorous, 'He was quite definitely and quite impenitently an escapist'. He had neither the conviction, nor the ruthless passion of a Swift. It might be said that Lytton Strachey opened veins, rather than severed arteries.

Max goes on to say 'Need we be angry?' and to give his happy reasons for rejoicing in Lytton Strachey's less drastic gifts. But he shows in the same moment that he lets him off—why also Lytton Strachey's great dramatic gifts have had to be used in a muffled, indirect way—rather than directly—since any escapist shrinks from the direct launching of his fullest powers.

Strachey never dared launch himself beyond the limits of history—even the characters he chose best had to be those emotionally disinfected eighteenth-century characters. When he tried 'Elizabeth' and the sixteenth-century characters surrounding her—there was not force enough in him to reach their passionate hearts.

Yet the dramatic heats up beneath the fear of it—as all our gifts haunt us—in spite of the limitations we enforce on them, through our lack of courage. How truthfully and tenderly Max points out to us, in Lytton's 'Queen Victoria', that the characters are interpreted in the changing style, as if the author slipped out of himself, to be in turn each one of them.

How gently, but with what a deadly felicity, Max Beerbohm shows up the fatal easiness of Dr. Joad's too fluent style, in comparison to the clear-cut luminosity of Strachey's.

There is no reproach, no sharp-tongued censure, but from the sentence beginning 'Not long ago I heard that agile and mellifluous quodlibetarian, Dr. Joad, saying in answer to a questioner, who wanted to write good letters, that anybody could write good letters: one had but to think out clearly what one wanted to say, and then set it down in the simplest terms—"to the inspired refutation—'A true gift for writing . . . is not widely bestowed. Nor is a true gift for painting, or for playing the violin; and of that we are somehow aware. We do not say to a violinist 'Just think out clearly what you want to express and then go straight ahead. Never mind how you handle your bow'. Nor to a painter, 'Got your subject and your scheme of colour in your head all right, eh? Then don't bother about how you lay your paints on, dear old boy'. Let us not make similar remarks to writers."

In this world of disciplined unflagging craftsmanship Max Beerbohm reigns supreme. He never confuses what should be paid to the Caesar of style—nor what should be paid to the God of creation.

His is no beauty 'off the point', it is beauty directly on it.

Yet is there not a sense in which we must feel that he too, is sometimes an escapist—perhaps a deeper one than Lytton Strachey whom he so skilfully exonerates? For Max Beerbohm is the distinguished exile, who has stepped too far away from that vital communication which lies between an author and his audience; feeding the life of the creative mind.

Max Beerbohm was never false to his morality; but what he gave was stinted in quantity; although its quality was always exquisite.

The fruit at the bottom of his basket is exactly as luscious and ripe as the fruit at the top. Yet he could have given more —if he had loved life more—and this is always a tragedy; not only for the world but for the creative artist himself. Max Beerbohm could not trust life further than he could see it; and life has to be trusted in order to prove itself trustworthy. So that there is a bitterness in the silence into which he sank out of sight and sound; and in his turning his back upon a world that still prizes him with a special favour, there is even a certain resentment. The last time he spoke upon the radio, a modern medium that he treasures and understands, so that to hear him speak on it is a quite peculiar pleasure; he spoke with inimitable but cruel ferocity. The gentle exquisite voice, first having recalled with a sort of icy regret the sound workers of the 'naughty nineties' (called 'naughty' because on the whole they were trying to become honest) changed, after full justice had been done them, into mockery—the cadenced tones became the clipped, tinny utterances of those vicariously intimate young ladies, who speak so far too often to us, on the B.B.C.

'Good night, children,' Max Beerbohm venomously murmured, with their exact shade of intrusive tenderness—'Good-night, children—everywhere.'

3

THE SECRET OF IVOR NOVELLO

Here is a man who has held enthralled an enormous public for a quarter of a century. What is his secret?

Ivor Novello was the only child of Welsh parents. Music poured out of them both; and he was the centre of their entire lives. Undoubtedly he was spoiled; but he was not *half*-spoiled as most children are, whose parents are largely responsible for making them disagreeable, and then turn round upon these helpless objects of their inept attention, and proceed to make them more disagreeable still—by disliking them. Ivor may have been *thoroughly* spoiled but it was by love; and by the love of parents who though they had no other object for their affections, had occupations which kept their pressure off him. The love of his Celtic parents often broke its precious balms over Ivor's head; but it always remained precious.

His mother, a dynamic character, made a highly successful career for herself. Her Welsh choir was famous all over the world; and many of her pupils became celebrities. She was herself a celebrity. Therefore, from the first, Ivor was brought up in an atmosphere of electric ambition working at high pressure and for desirable results. Work, hard work spurred on by equally hard excitement was the air he breathed. Scenes were part of his daily bread; and reconcilements were his butter. His father, a Cardiff Corporation Official, had an active temperament, personal beauty and a sharply puncturing will of his own. But his mother was Ivor's main young influence; and it is to her that he owes an abiding sense of ardour and achievement.

She loved him wildly and often unwisely. Fortunately she

moved about in a world larger than her home. Her heart was her child's but her strong will was largely spent in becoming Madam Novello Davies the renowned—perhaps the most renowned—singing teacher in Great Britain. Had Ivor been her only object in life, as well as her only son, he might very well have wrecked himself against her strong will, and passionate maternal instinct; but the very fact that she had to adjust Ivor's wants to her career, saved the child from complete saturation. Ivor wrung himself dry in the intervals of her tenderness, and devoted himself to his own affairs.

It might have been supposed that music would have been Ivor's path to glory. He possessed all the necessary gifts for it.

As a Magdalen choir boy, he sang with the voice of an angel; and if imagination is to be trusted about angels—with the appearance of one. He soon became chief solo boy and was trained thoroughly, as choir boys are trained in such a school as M.C.S. to understand the elements of music.

Ivor has never had one of those rightly distrusted temperaments, falsely called 'artistic'; he is not one of those fake-artists, who are only prepared with the emotions, never with the essentials, of their art. Ivor neither expected nor even wished to take things easy; nor on the other hand has he belonged to that race of moral stoics who prefer to take things hard. Where he wanted to do anything well, he took the trouble to learn how to do it; where any job was indifferent or antipathetic to him, he took equal trouble to avoid learning it.

Nature was more or less at his disposal but she would have been less docile to him, had he not possessed the necessary courage to tackle her secrets.

All his life Ivor has been completely at home with music; but it was never his goal.

Even when his angelic soprano voice changed into a flexible and highly sympathetic baritone, Ivor refused the career of a singer, because he felt that he could never have been an important one. 'I would far rather', he has said, 'hear people say "why *doesn't* Ivor sing?" than "why *does* he?" ' From the age of seventeen, Ivor had only to sit at a piano with words that appealed to him put before him (and most words appealed to him) to turn them into original and enchanting melodies.

His greatest friend, himself deeply musical, yearned to see Ivor become a future Schubert or even Mozart, and urged him towards serious musical composition, but a strange flaw cracked the jewel of Ivor's composer talent. The more he concentrated upon the technique of composition, the swifter the power and sweetness of his melodies evaporated. Something within himself winced away from the intricacies of construction. He made music as a bird sings, not as a thinker thinks. His was the genius of a troubadour. Perhaps the reason for this evasion—for it was a voluntary evasion on Ivor's part, not lack of talent—may have been that music was his mother's field. She had succeeded in it. Few children care to follow in the footsteps of a successful parent. The shadow of the tree above them threatens their dawning light.

Outwardly there was no failure, on the contrary as a young composer Ivor was a prodigy of success, though his flights were short. While still in his teens he produced two songs, familiar all over England. 'Keep the Home fires burning' was the most popular, but within Ivor the fires of his own being had already taken a different direction. He proposed to keep his own fires burning well outside the Home.

The theatre was his lifelong aim. Once more success seemed easy. The stage could not but accept his young beauty, his musical gifts, his infectious charm.

Certainly he could be a successful actor, but here again there was a still more curious flaw; and a very unexpected one. His face was his misfortune. Ivor was tripped up by his beauty. All he had to do on the stage was to present his profile and smile—the Public did the rest. He became an idol; and idols are dangerous to themselves as well as to their worshippers. A great actor must be an actor first and an idol afterwards; but Ivor was instantly an idol and this checked for many years his powers as an actor. Perhaps too the heady drama of being caught up into the highest circle of London's Bright Young Things, hindered his concentration at a vital moment. They took him up with rapture, fleeced him like cormorants, and clung to him like leeches. But they did not get the chance, usually presented to them by their victims, of sucking Ivor dry and then throwing him away into complete oblivion. Ivor soon saw into what a gulf of selfish emptiness they were prepared to fling his vitality—his power of creating drama—his warm and true affections.

They even expected him to pay for their fun; and he learned that besides paying for it, he must provide it. He *was* in fact their fun; and it was upon his spontaneous heart that they proposed to nourish the worn-out uncreative organs of their own. They wanted both his money and his life. Wasn't darling Ivor, they said to themselves, earning heaps of money by his clever productions, while they—poor impecunious grandees—had to exist on their mere names, their families and any rich dupe they could persuade to foot their bills? It was the sapping of his *powers*, rather than the money their expensive pleasures cost him, that Ivor had the sense to grudge. But it was a grudge that he never revealed to them. There was no open quarrel, he simply became more and more inaccessible. He faded away with the good-natured celerity of Lewis Carroll's famous Snark, and for the same reason—'For the Snark *was* a Boojum, you see'. Ivor was intrinsically an artist and not a bright young thing. When they telephoned, Ivor was never at the receiver. When they wrote, there were no answering letters. Here and there among them Ivor had found a friendship that seemed worth keeping; and these he holds to this day. When he came across the others he met them with the old enchanting friendliness, but he did not meet them often—or for long. Ivor had deep in his blood the worker's contempt for idleness; not for that highly-seasoned mess of pottage—Social Life—would he reject his birthright!

Perhaps Ivor had always been loved too much, even at home, and had learned in his early years the technique of withdrawing just enough to be able to breathe when necessary. He was well accustomed to being pursued and besieged by eager and not always very generous lovers.

The hearts he broke became the talk of London. But some

of them were unduly brittle; nor had Ivor always asked to be pursued. He was himself an eager and a generous lover; but he rarely consolidated his victories.

His was the tragedy of many sons who have been loved too well. Nothing could now satisfy him but the heart of a middle-aged woman in the body of a young girl. Alas! it is easy enough to find the heart of a young girl in the body of a middle-aged woman; but nature seems to baulk at uniting maturity with the charms of youth.

Ivor has not yet found what he sought for, and perhaps he is looking for it still.

The crudities of his contemporaries could not satisfy him; he was too accustomed to being the adored companion of a mature woman of great strength, who devoted to his every interest the concentrated passion of a panther.

Lovely, trivial butterflies exacting Ivor's attention, simply hampered his work. Their calls upon his time and his creative energies came too late; and into a life that had never been exposed to such calls. As for the older women who besieged his heart; it had never been theirs—for that particular purpose. Ivor was delighted with their affection, and always prepared to return it with interest; but, not on any account whatever, did he want their passions on his doorstep. What he wanted was to turn on his gramophone, and share a cup of cocoa with them.

Ivor had the deepest, tenderest affection for all his older friends—but he was not anxious to make love to them. He was merely ready to enjoy the ready-made love he found, in his own way. Alas! it was not always their way and the point at issue was generally insoluble. Ivor was neither idle nor a roué. He was a worker; and he was constant. All his life for instance he was true to the love he felt for Viola Tree and Constance Collier; and to many far less famous men and women. But these two women were his friends of friends. Perhaps younger women objected to their influence over him; if they did they lost Ivor—for he could not change. Half his fireside was Eddie Marsh, but even Eddie was only half a fireside.

Ivor had many intimates, male and female, dear and constant, but he was—and remains—a Peter Pan.

Yet it is doubtful if Ivor wished to avoid the main obligations of life. He had no vicious tendencies—perhaps he had no tendencies at all! But he would not have been averse from domesticity had Psyche not always dropped—at the critical moment—hot wax upon his wings.

Ivor was curiously ready to accept lesser human obligations. At one time he kept seventeen constant dependents of his own or his parents. When he was the proud possessor of three successful shows in London, running at the same time, these tremendous generosities were easy to carry, but when less good days dawned, Ivor never dreamed of getting rid of them. Everyone simply went on, with less all round—including Ivor.

He had a real spiritual integrity which he never violated; and could show most unexpected firmness. He had a strong dislike of alcoholic excess. Even when he was surrounded by the Bright Young Things, he was himself strictly temperate. Yet he is not in the least dogmatic about alcohol. He supplies it for others but avoids it for himself.

During the period of his retreat from Fashion, his friend Constance Collier was of great practical assistance to him. She was herself a first-class actress; a splendid organizer and a woman of the world with a heart. From her and with her, he started writing his own plays, and began to act convincingly. From her too perhaps he learned how to hold his own in a dubious world of agents and theatrical middlemen.

Probably there has never been anyone on the stage who made as much money as Ivor, spent it as generously, or who was less cheated while earning it. If he owed much of this wisdom of his world to Constance Collier, he also owed a great deal to his own native common sense and to his brilliant handling of human beings. After all he had learned how to handle his own Celtic parents very early in life and they had not been an easy proposition!

His ability as an actor—as well as his phenomenal successes as a playwright—date from the period when he forsook

Society. He dived below the surface now, and everything that he learned from the great world he had thrown over, went into his new and greater world.

Ivor had always had a great deal of taste—not all of it good—but now he began to use it with developing power upon production. Here again his personality reinforced his intellect. All his qualities of infectious courage, ruthless common sense and open-hearted friendliness leap out of his plays. His huge audiences are whirled away on the tides of his enthusiastic gaiety, and warmed to the core of their hearts by the sunshine of his friendliness. At last Ivor found a circle of friends who did not expect him to pay for his fun as well as to provide it. Ivor has never suffered from the Ananias and Sapphira complex. He gives what he has, and keeps back nothing; perhaps that is why he earns so much money; is so seldom cheated—and is so greatly loved.

Jealous men and women have no doubt tormented and deceived him, but he has drowned out all his private bitternesses in the deep rich stream of his friendship with the world.

It would however be a mistake to suppose that the devotion of his Public gives Ivor less work than other actors find necessary—it gives him more. Whatever is wrong upon the stage, if a carpet won't fit; if a leading lady bursts her wide prerogatives into open tyranny, Ivor's wit finds the solutions. The carpet fits, the lady yields; the play goes on. When anything or anyone becomes too obstreperous for his easy genius to master he falls back upon his ruthless common sense. Has he not the fire of his own Welsh temper to use as a weapon? If anyone has got to be nasty—well—can't Ivor be a little nastier? He can—he is—terror reigns—order is at length restored! But Ivor won't be nasty if he can help it. He has no foundation of bad temper. Discouragement—that fount of malice—has never flung him into the stagnant pool of envy and self pity. He seldom has the least desire to hurt anyone's feelings.

All his Company knows that they get a square deal from Ivor plus something on the top of it—a bonus of good will. Working for Ivor, they have the special sense of being at rather more than their best. They will be *more* appreciated, and *more* applauded into the bargain, and rather better paid, than had they been working for anyone else.

The writer once—many years ago, watched Ivor for a day and a half shooting the film of *The Constant Nymph* in Bavaria. It was, as all good films are, a difficult production. People who knew nothing about dogs were trying to produce a scene with a highly-strung Alsatian. Several of the most attractive girls were in love with Ivor; and not in full harmony with each other. The Producer (Ivor was merely the hero of the film) was in an unspeakable temper—indeed he literally could not trust himself to open his mouth—and it would have been much better if he had *not* trusted himself before he shut it—had retired to his room where his meals were carried to him on a tray. Nobody knew German, yet all the mechanics in a Bavarian Studio could only speak German. There was some trouble with the singing. An elderly actress with an important role had been seriously upset by one of the younger actresses.

Everyone wanted Ivor to take his or her part against everyone else. Ivor did not take anyone's part and yet he appeared to take everyone's. He gave sympathy and undogmatic love-making to the besieging young ladies. He played and sang enchanting will-o'-the-wisp snatches of songs when awful pauses fell upon the studio—after the Alsatian, for instance, bit one of the men who did not understand it. Later on, Ivor managed with infinite adroitness to unloose the rigidity of the Producer. He entirely re-composed the elderly actress; he slowly unwound the intricacies of a foreign tongue. Nor did Ivor call it a day, till he had treated the whole Company to a remarkably hair-raising switchback; and the joy of a rink where blunt-nosed imitation motors could batter each other murderously; and with impunity.

Ivor knows, as few other actor-managers have ever known, how to make things work. To every part of his vast productions he contributed something. No detail is too small for him, no difficulty is insurmountable. He gives to the play a writer's eye for a scene and the singer's ear for dialogue. To the part he gives an actor's sincerity; to the company he manages, a human being's sympathy and understanding.

Perhaps his public senses this warm universality of talents and realizes the compliment paid to it, by Ivor's determined mastery of things both material and immaterial. It is certain that he retains the permanent loyalty of the British Public. Many actors have been adored over long periods; many artists have been famous all their working lives. Beautiful men and women have held undisputed sway over a susceptible public—while their beauty lasted; but 'Beauty vanishes, beauty passes; However rare—rare it be'. Ivor's beauty has not vanished, although a quarter of a century is a long run for your money! There are even some of us who prefer the enchanting smile, the radiant eyes, the well-loved face with the marks of life upon it, to the same face when it was soft and young and with the bloom of youth. They prefer, too, what is behind the face.

The acid test of Ivor Novello both as a human being and as an artist came with the outbreak of war in 1939.

What should Ivor—over age for active service, but far too young for any evasion of personal responsibility—do to help his country?

Ivor has often been doubted as an artist, but he possesses one quality—perhaps the highest that any artist can possess—he knows his duty to his public. When the Hour struck, he was instantly ready to risk fame, future, life itself in order to carry out his duty.

The Government, Ivor fondly hoped, might like the services of that magnificent entertainment *The Dancing Years*—then at its peak in London—for the Forces. He and his Company were willing to forgo any great financial success if they could help amuse and sustain their country's fighters. The correct department was sought. Ivor's offer was received by Basil Dean with the greatest enthusiasm—they would be used, he was told, at the first opportunity. Time rolled by. Apparently there was no 'first opportunity' for the entertainment of the Forces—not at least for a first-rate entertainment.

Ivor was faced with the alternative—equally unpleasant—

to disband the entire Company on an empty market—or to risk the whole of his future by putting *The Dancing Years* on the Road. He could of course retire in perfect comfort and financial security to his cottage in the country, there to await the indeterminate 'call' of his country's officials for his separate services—though what has a great producer to serve with—other than his production?

Ivor chose the road, partly for his Company's sake and partly because he would not turn his back upon the People who loved him.

The capital value of *The Dancing Years* as composed of its original cast, costs, costumes, and running expenses, was half a million pounds. The whole of this sum might be lost in one night by 'enemy action' on the road. It might be lost too —if Ivor were ill—for without his presence the years would not have danced.

It was a prodigal decision; but Ivor took it, and it was justified as only a generous giver is ever justified. *The Dancing Years* played 601 times in fourteen cities, chiefly raided cities outside London. The play drew an audience of 15,000 people weekly. It kept 80 actors and 24 staff—none of them physically suited for the forces—on the job instead of on the dole. The Treasury must have benefited considerably by this unaided private venture. But its chief value was what *The Dancing Years* gave to the British Public. All through the worst raid-shaken weeks of 1940–41—in bombed and agitated cities—all over this threatened, ill-protected island, this very apposite, half gay, half tragic drama gave itself, to nourish the spirit and the imagination of the British people. It was in truth 'a food convenient for them', and there was no mistaking what they thought of it.

In Sunderland, that grim, hard-working town, still turning out yearly the greatest number of ships of any city in the world—they had never had a big show for fifteen years; but they had one now, and Ivor and his gallant Company played to audiences that brought in £2,600 a week—to prove how they liked it. Ivor and his company went to battered Hull, to Liverpool—almost nightly harrowed—to Birmingham and

Bristol, while the great raids tore them. Every night they took their chance; and how they travelled in between! Sometimes the Company spent fourteen hours in a train without either food or heating, on a four and a half hour's run. Sometimes the trains they travelled in were machine gunned from the air. Often the actors tramped through black-outs in the rain, searching for lodgings for anxious hours in strange cities. Even when found, the lodgings were sometimes only a made-up bed in a bathroom, or a couple of chairs in a crowded front-parlour; or when a raid was on, a mere shaken rest, in an air-raid shelter. A hundred and four persons cannot be booked for in advance in war-time. But Ivor and his company —the pampered darlings of London audiences—stuck it like heroes for seventy uninterrupted weeks. They could take no holidays for they dared not break up and re-form this huge piece of theatrical business, of which Ivor bore the greater part on his own shoulders. A sore throat, a sprained ankle, a private grief at any moment might upset the whole show. The Minister of Production withdrew Ivor's understudy and treated Ivor as if he were trying to undermine war-production, so little can even a good man, in a hurry, value the enormous auxiliary powers of the roused imagination. In *The Dancing Years*, the war workers could see for themselves the ravage the Nazis had made of easy, happy, spirit-loving Austria, and they could see that only courage and good-will could outwit and outlast the crass stupidity of Force!

For months Ivor slept on a financial precipice if not with unruffled calm, with incredible optimism. The Play went on, and was everywhere received with the same release and joy of the human spirit.

Nothing disastrous occurred in the Provinces and at last the welcoming arms of the Adelphi opened to receive *The Dancing Years* again, and bag and baggage the wanderers returned to their home. Then the blow struck, first the leading lady, then Ivor himself became victims of a dangerous type of influenza leading to pneumonia. It would not be an exaggeration to say that during Ivor's illness the blood of his entire Company: his devoted household; his nearest friends —ran cold.

His Company may have been like other threatened companies when he was well. Suffering occasionally the pangs and penalties of envy and jealousy. Did not Ivor—even if he ran the *greatest* risk, reap the greatest reward? No doubt in normal times they grumbled with and without reason, made scenes, unlike the cheerful ones prepared for an audience. They may even have bitten bits out of Ivor's reputation behind his adored back. Actors and actresses are but human, but Ivor menaced; and they knew that the 'back' *was* adored. Ivor, they all realized, was not like any other leading actor and producer. He was Ivor. He did not save the Company for the sake of making money out of them. He had tried to save them when he might have lost every penny he possessed, in the effort to save them. They were his 'family' and he had always given them that warm first-hand protection and consideration due to a man's children. What his Company gave to Ivor in return, when he was struck down by his dangerous illness, can be guessed from the abandon and fresh vitality, they were ready to put into *The Dancing Years* when he returned to them. All of them wanted a new play. Ivor had one ready down to the last detail, but London could never have enough of *The Dancing Years*. So the play goes on to this hour that I write; and Ivor and his fellow-workers in the theatre still await their release into fresh pastures; obeying with spontaneous zest, their primary duty of giving the Public what it wants.

It is interesting to compare Ivor Novello's fame with that of his brilliant contemporary, Noel Coward.

Ivor has less wit than Noel; but whereas Noel's wit springs from cold intellectual gaiety, Ivor's is a warmer, briefer wit springing from the heart. As an actor Ivor is the better man, he draws far larger houses, and is better loved. He has more facets to his nature to *be* loved. Noel Coward with a more concentrated intelligence, has produced better plays with a less wide appeal: with one exception, for the British Navy struck at the core of Noel Coward's imagination

—and he produced, with his heart as well as with his mind, the film *In which we serve*.

Noel Coward is a brilliant, sophisticated, bored, witty man-about-town, and this is what he is on the stage; but Ivor is a human being—he is himself and everyone else as well. Noel Coward could not play the 'Rat', but there were moments in the 'Rat' as a gangster—when Ivor nearly breaks two of his 'Moll's' wrists; slouches about his nightclub den, or flings himself in desperation against his prison door;—far surpassing in sheer force and naturalness any of his contemporaries. Ivor can be—indeed he *is*—a great actor. In the *Happy Hypocrite* he fairly astonished London by his 'Lord George Hell', a ruthless, tasteless, truculent rake of the eighteenth century. Ivor makes a perfectly natural, sympathetic Viennese musician in *The Dancing Years*; as well as a subtle brilliantly played oriental in *Careless Rapture*—who defies you not to believe he is a Chinaman. When Ivor acted 'Henry the Fifth' in London, at a moment of political appeasement, to an audience that was not asking to be turned into heroes either by Shakespeare or by Ivor Novello, he played the King with such passion and intensity, that the members of his audience very nearly became heroes in spite of themselves.

As a playwright, Noel Coward undoubtedly produces plays of more intellectual value than Ivor's; but there is something about Ivor's that makes them—as well as highly popular at the moment—strangely endearing. His plays have a vitality, a movement, a sincerity that catches the Public eye with a sense of infectious gaiety. Nor is this popularity only due to the fact that they are sure to end well (though there is a large number of any audience who prefer this limitation to art) but because the whole audience is sure of a sort of rhythm of good-fellowship. Joy—not only the destinies of human beings—is going to come out top.

Never need Ivor Novello say like the poet Shelley—'Rarely—rarely comest thou, Spirit of Delight!' In almost everything he writes or sings, or says or does, this 'Spirit of Delight' gleams and beckons to his audience—at once an invitation and an ecstasy.

The author has seen him act in plays which she must—as works of art—deplore. But even when the curses rose unbidden to her lips—she found herself suddenly forced to replace them by blessings—'A light that never was on sea or land' had intervened. Ivor had done it again!

There is a moment in the life of every true artist when—in a flash—he knows he has done well to be an artist. Whatever failures beset him, whatever doom eventually befalls him, he has been repaid for all.

In this one blinding significant moment he sees that he has got what he desired—and deserved what he has got.

This moment came to Ivor when he was asked by the Foreign Office, to be one of the six chosen musicians of Great Britain, who were to write a song for the Underground Movement of Europe.

Ivor was both astounded and enchanted at being chosen even as one of the six; and when the Committee of fourteen experts, drawn from the Allied European Missions in this country, unanimously chose his song—then his cup was full.

The Voters did not know the names of the six candidates. They heard each song record played twice on the gramophone, and then voted for the number they preferred.

When the last song had been played for the second time, the Judges—ignoring the pens and papers laid before them—shouted in unison Ivor's number: 'three'.

The passion of sympathy and admiration that had stirred his Welsh heart for the voiceless heroes of the Underground Movement had made his music the most alive.

The great servant of the Public had used his own heart to reach—and therefore *had* reached—hearts that were not his own.

Just as in the early days of Ivor's first youth and beauty, when he took London by storm, the crowds still wait for him at the stage door. Some of the faces are long familiar to him over a space of years; to those he gives friendly words and the touch of his hand. Others are strangers, but he smiles at them; and they are no longer strangers. He is tired, but he never hurries through that waiting throng to go home to his rest, because he knows that his real home is with each one of them.

The British Public has loved Ivor Novello faithfully for more than a quarter of a century; and it is not a habit that they are ever likely to give up, because they have discovered the secret of his life—Ivor is in love with *them*!

4

SARA DELANO ROOSEVELT

When Sara Delano Roosevelt died, it was not only the end of a long and valuable life, it was the breaking-up of a human mould.

There will never be any more Mrs. James D. Roosevelts. Sara was unique; the very materials and habits out of which such women made themselves, no longer exist.

Sara Delano was a Social Presence—perhaps *the* Social Presence of the United States of America.

Throughout the country, from coast to coast, among her son's worst enemies as well as among his most devoted friends, Sara Delano Roosevelt stood as a symbol of absolute integrity. In exactly the sense that Caesar's wife wasn't, Sara Delano *was*, above suspicion. She had dignity, she had grace; she had the certainty of acting upon her own convictions.

Once, when I was combating one of the many silly and scurrilous lies told about the President by those of his political opponents who found the truth unpalatable, the storyteller rounded upon me and said, 'Well—I'll only believe my story isn't true if Mrs. James D. Roosevelt herself writes and denies it!' I answered, 'Will her bare word be sufficient to convince you?' The young man answered with some heat, 'Her word's good enough for any decent American!' He received Sara Delano Roosevelt's word by return of post, and I hope had sufficient sporting sense to repudiate his story. But what an unlimited and splendid personal reputation the President's mother must have won for herself, when even the rank hostility of political prejudice bowed down before her!

Sara Delano was one of the three beautiful Delano sisters. I do not know if she was the most beautiful; she herself insisted that she was the least; but she had beauty all her life, both of an inner and an outer kind.

She was born into a household of plenty; plenty of money; plenty of education; plenty of good taste and kindliness; and she never at first-hand, knew anything else. It would have been difficult for Sara Delano to be, or to believe in, any other type of good woman. Not that she would for a moment have agreed with Tennyson's 'Farmer' that 'the Poor in a lump are bad'; but the facts upon which the morals of poor and uneducated people are based, were not part of her actual experience.

She had great compassion for those less well off than herself, but not that complete understanding which can come only from fellow-suffering.

Her ideal of goodness for her sex consisted in a limited, but inexorable, set of virtues—beginning with chastity as a corner stone. Not Joan of Arc, could have passed into Sara Delano's good graces without chastity. This, Sara expected of every woman, however great—however humble. Sara might at a pinch, have admitted that a good King could possess a mistress; but she would *never* have admitted thata good Queen might possess a lover. Perhaps at the further end of the scale Sara Roosevelt would have forgiven a starving girl for selling her virtue, but Sara would never have thought the same of her as of a starving girl who didn't.

The other virtues which she thought women should possess are less easy to define, and could at times be allowed to yield to the Law of Relativity. But such tolerance was for others. What made Sara Delano Roosevelt a great woman, was that she showed no such tolerance to herself. What she believed in, she was; and her country did well to honour her for the grace of her consistency. If she had been less severe with herself, she might have remained a great Lady, but she would not have been—as in fact she was—a great woman.

Throughout history, great sons have been the fruit of greatness in their mothers. This may have been specially true when the only greatness a woman was allowed to possess was in what she was able to hand on to her children. Sara Delano had no other ideal for women. She thought of them as carrying out their mission to the world only when they devoted every power and virtue they possessed, to the care and well-being of husband and child.

This limitation of woman's sphere to the home probably accounts for her almost morbid horror of divorce—shared by her brilliant and enchanting sister, Dora Delano Forbes. I remember, as a young married woman, asking 'Dora' if I might come to see her alone. She was my husband's 'marraine', and he was in the French trenches at the time so that I was specially anxious to talk to her about him; and we usually met through a mist of other people. She turned upon me with a flash of horrified fear in her eyes. 'What!' she exclaimed, 'do *you* want to talk to me about—are you thinking of getting a divorce?' When I assured her that this was the last idea in my mind at the moment, she instantly apologized and said, 'Please forgive me—but if you knew *how* afraid I always am of hearing such stories from my friends! I am obliged to listen if such events take place in my own family, or that of my husband's! But I need not hear them, need I—from my friends as well?'

Sara would have shared her sister Dora's horror, but she might have consented to listen.

A divorce simply meant to them both the complete failure of a woman's life. All that they had set out to be, all that they had actually achieved, was at stake in the matter. Every thought, every wish, every plan, of Sara's heart had been thrown with single-minded zeal, into the perfection of her own home-making.

The husband she adored had been snatched from her by death, in their early middle age; upon her son therefore the full concentration of her heart was based. He was to her a lighted torch, which it was her duty to hand on from one generation to another.

Perhaps Sara Delano Roosevelt was the happiest woman in the world, for she lived to see all her highest hopes fulfilled, her standards kept; her wisdom justified in the career of her only child. She could look back upon a marriage as nearly perfect as an imperfect human being can expect. 'I still think my husband the greatest man who ever lived!' she said, after her son had been elected President for the second time; but she said it with a no less unswerving and steadfast devotion to her son.

When a friend said to her, 'It must make you happy to hear such wonderful praises of your son!' she answered with an enchanting smile, 'Yes, but you see, I always knew Franklin was like that—it is no news to me!'

In order to make the contribution she had set herself to make towards the wellbeing of her husband and child, Sara Delano became a great deal more than what the world accepted her as being—the leader of New York society.

This goal was important to her, and she liked to know that she had won it; but it was never the aim of her life. It was a mere secondary flowering of a great personality whose heart was set upon a fundamental value that had nothing to do with the world.

Sara Delano Roosevelt was rich; both her family, and her husband's, were well born, well connected, and instrumental in developing the life of their country. Sara took all these things for granted—very pleasantly for granted. They were her realities. She moved among them, behaving as she considered such benefits exacted; but she never identified herself with society. Society belonged to her; but Sara never belonged to it. She belonged heart and soul to her home.

She merely trained herself to use all the advantages her position gave to her to further her singleminded aim—the complete wellbeing of her husband and son.

In order to succeed in this object, she demanded from herself the greatest thing that can be demanded from any of us; she determined to become a good human being. Whatever she had to sacrifice in order to become her idea of a good human being, Sara Delano willingly sacrificed.

Her greatness consisted in the fact that she became one. In her own field, and within the radius of the light she walked by, Sara Delano Roosevelt was as reliable as the rock of ages.

She did not however, win the position she held in New

York society simply by being good. She happened to be beautiful as well as good, and filled to the brim by an entertaining spirit.

Sara, as Thoreau tells us the 'Innocent' do, 'enjoyed the story'. Whatever came over the horizon of her daily life, she met with welcome and resilience. She gave herself to all 'the changes and chances of this wicked world' with simplicity and generosity; and with that special grace that was her own.

There could not have been a dull occasion in any house where she was a guest; and as a hostess, Sara Roosevelt was as easy and natural as sunlight. She liked to laugh, and was ready to enjoy any kind of humour that did not shock her well-known prejudices.

But beyond her humour—the very seat and secret of her being—spread her geniality. She was readier to like than to dislike any stranger. She only asked of people that they should be well bred and socially harmonious; then she quickly invested them with all the deeper virtues she had set her soul upon, and must have been flabbergasted when—as sometimes happened—these radical virtues were not to be found beneath the shining surface.

Sara Roosevelt had all the unreasonable social prejudices of her day; but they were always less deep than her loyalties. Like the social triumphs which she took so ungraspingly, she could let these prejudices go if any deeper reason of the heart bade her give them up. When the Nazi persecution of the Jews began to spread its cruel and insidious poison over the United States, Sara Delano was too chivalrous and honest by nature not to side instantly with the persecuted. She had a strong social prejudice against Jews; but she waived this aside and instantly sprang to their rescue. 'If you say such things in my house, my dear,' she told an anti-Semite friend, who was bitterly attacking the Chosen People, 'I shall never call you a Christian again—why, you're nothing but a Gentile!'

Part of her undisputed leadership in the social world, Sara Delano owed to her moral courage. She would never allow unkindness to take place in her presence.

Strict as were her own morals, she had far too good a heart and far too just a spirit, not to make every allowance for the individual case.

Nor was she, in the baser sense of the word, snobbish. It is true that she preferred her world to be peopled by others of her own class, who spoke her own language, appreciated her ideals, and had been brought up with similar habits. But rank and money, as such, had no attractions for her unless they were combined with the qualities she thought they ought to represent. If people didn't behave as Sara thought they should, not all the fortune of Midas, nor the blood of a thousand dynasties, would have for a moment improved them in the eyes of Sara Delano.

When she went to tea with King George and Queen Mary of England, she enjoyed them for being kind, good people who shared her interests—not for being King George or Queen Mary. She expected them to be what she found they were, and that was enough for her. When she entertained King George VI and Queen Elizabeth at Hyde Park, her reactions were the same. It pleased her to entertain Kings and Queens on a visit; but they had to be good ones. Hitler—even if he owned the earth—would never have been allowed inside Mrs. James Roosevelt's drawing-room.

The love she had made her whole life, was concentrated upon her family; but nevertheless it spread out in shining ripples into the lives of all her friends. Sara Roosevelt shared their interests; she took what she could from their burdens. She sparkled over their joys as if they were her own.

She had as a daughter-in-law a woman as dynamic as herself, but wholly different in temperament and outlook. In fact probably the only thing these two great women had in common was that they were both good; but even their goodness was essentially different in quality.

Sara Delano Roosevelt based all her ideals upon the standards of yesterday. Some of those ideals, it is true, had a universal and permanent value; but Sara Roosevelt, like all her generation of sheltered and male-protected women, had no knowledge of how these ideals could or should be applied universally—whereas Eleanor Roosevelt moved in a changing world towards universal brotherhood.

Sara Roosevelt was a Democrat because she was a good American but she belonged to the Hamiltonian, rather than to the Jeffersonian, type of Democrat.

The wife and the mother of one of the world's greatest leaders must often have had to look at the same things; but they must have seen them with very different eyes. It is greatly to the credit of both that they made constant adjustments throughout the long years when they were thrown together in perhaps the most difficult intimacy the human family provides; and each ended by feeling for the other a deep and sincere respect. Fortunately each was endowed with good manners and good humour, as well as trained in iron self control; and they may both have found plenty of opportunities for such qualities.

When a mother's relationship with an only child is also that of an only parent, a daughter-in-law can never find her path an easy one, while the mother invariably feels deprived by a younger woman with a stronger claim, of many of her rights and privileges. Grandchildren too, can be used both as a tie—and as a weapon. Whatever else they are likely to be—and however dearly loved—grandchildren cannot be expected to see eye to eye with two generations behind them.

Mrs. Roosevelt loved all her grandchildren, but she did not agree with them. 'After all,' she would say with her sweet shrewd smile, 'they *are* Franklin's children—not mine. Of course I love them, but Franklin stands alone!'

Sara Roosevelt lived to a great age; but she never grew old. She remained, to the end, interested, genial, open to the least hint of her old ally—Life. She would not have a secretary, a companion or a nurse for those last long years. She heightened her independence and her loneliness. She was not afraid of anything, nor of anyone. Everything she had planned had come right; everything she had believed in, she believed in still. She had given herself ungrudgingly to the world in which she found herself, and had maintained its standards. She had had her share of sorrows; and one overwhelming grief; but Sara Roosevelt knew that she was highly favoured. The past, the present and the future alike, blessed her; and received in return her unequivocal blessing.

She had never been separated from her son by a thought. She had not controlled him—except by her love. She had not attempted to guide him for many years; but she had made him. This was her life—and this relationship with him was what made her, in her friends' opinion, the happiest woman in the world.

The last few years of her life, Sara Roosevelt drew back from the world—as the Almighty is said to have withdrawn from the earth after the long chaos of creation. Sara, too, rested; and for the same reason. She rested because she saw that what she had created was good.

5

EZRA POUND

In the history of twentieth-century Literature Ezra Pound may be known and valued more as a Portent than as a Poet. He was one of those unfortunate swallows who arrive early, but do not make a summer. Yet I think he had in him the making of many summers.

A quarter of a century ago he was saying to a predatory and complacent world what every young person and most intelligent older ones now automatically believe. Yet nobody believed the youthful Ezra when he first preached his creed of objective art, and urged the intellectual necessity of being as honest as you can be, and as direct as you had better train yourself to know how to be. If the proof of being right is endurance, the Idolino in the Etruscan Museum in Florence, after a thousand years, is still right. To be wholly right would be to endure for ever; but to be even considerably right, well ahead of your generation, is to confer an elixir of youth upon oneself.

The notable fact about Ezra Pound's criticism (and his genius was predominatingly critical) is that it so seldom dates. But the unfortunate part of his vituperative pronouncements is that though so often right, he was, when wrong, so very wrong indeed; and so easily proved so by Pedants far more exact, and less dynamically creative than he was himself. If his brilliant intellect had been a little more patient, and a little less vitriolic, his 'day' would have been longer, and far easier for himself.

The evil that men do lives after them,
The good is oft interred with their bones.

Yet perhaps Mark Antony was speaking ironically when he made this pessimistic statement. Like most paradoxes, it can be turned the other way round with equal truth. As far as Ezra is concerned, I like to think he will be forgotten as the belligerent sycophant of Fascism and remembered as what he was when I first knew him, in the years before our little war of 1914, when he was trying to take London by storm.

Foreigners always find that a difficult process—in fact only one of them made a real success of it—and Disraeli possessed what Ezra had been denied—the elasticity and toughness of a good Jew.

Ezra had neither toughness nor elasticity; he was as rigidly intelligent as a Plymouth brother; and as vulnerable as a sea-anemone.

His unquiet personality could not outface the somnolent arrogance of the greatest city in the world.

Yet Britain needed the youthful Ezra, almost as much as Ezra needed the thickly padded hide of this favoured country—'the envy of unhappier lands'. Ezra when not drunk on Fascist propaganda knew that truth was Everyman's business; and that Everyman should and could be trained to understand it. He was also one of the first of the moderns to understand that man could make himself—if he knew how—and rather better than he has let himself be made.

When I first met Ezra, at a literary tea-party given by May Sinclair in pre-war London, he made the impression on me of an electric eel flung into a mass of flaccid substances. Physically he was a tall, slight, nervous young fellow, with the face of a scholarly satyr, red-gold hair, and a pointed beard of the same colour. Leonardo da Vinci might have used him equally well as a model for a cynical Christ with his eyes open; or for a spiritual and not wholly covetous Judas. Ezra was an intensely uncomfortable young man, even to himself, but he was most stimulating.

He never sat still for a moment; he endangered every chair he sat on; he had a most irritating staccato voice, and a short unnecessary cough which he wielded like a weapon. But every word he said had a meaning; and a meaning that very often had not occurred to anyone but himself.

Nor was Ezra (vain though he may have been) ever one of those stationary Narcissi contentedly gazing at his own reflection in a pool. His was the hunter's mind—always preoccupied by the quarry—seldom preoccupied by himself. He welcomed, fostered and encouraged intellect whenever he came across it. He was a generous-hearted and good-natured fellow who hungered to be (what he despised) a benevolent despot, ruling everyone intellectually for their own good.

In the short, but to me extraordinarily vitalizing interval of our acquaintance, I owed Ezra Pound three unforgettable first-hand experiences. He introduced me to the first really good meal I ever tasted; and I think that he gave it to me at a time when providing good meals for other people must have involved a certain amount of personal privation. He knew where the best things in London, gastronomic or artistic, were to be found; and he was always prepared to reveal and share them.

The second experience I owed to Ezra was even more valuable, though perhaps at the moment less palatable—Ezra gave me the first unbiased and objective literary criticism I had ever known. I still listen to this criticism, and that it has increased in value with every year of my growth, says something perhaps for its young creator. Although we were the same age almost to a month, the world of my youthful mind was at least a quarter of a century behind Ezra's.

'What are you?' Ezra impatiently once demanded. 'I can't make out. You seem to me a modern without a foundation; and a romantic without a roof!'

It was a just criticism, for I had successfully entered, at seventeen, precocious, and without a standard, the market of a profession which was at the time I stormed it, financially profitable rather than intellectually exacting. Ezra provided me with a standard; and gingered me into an attempt to train towards it. Three of his searchlight exactitudes stuck in me with the undeflectable poise of St. Sebastian's arrows.

1. 'A work of art is the honest reproduction of a concrete

image. Imagination is the faculty which finds out every fact about this image, and never the revelation of the feelings aroused by it.'

2. 'Why are you not content with saying that a man stepped intentionally upon a kitten? Surely it is not necessary to add that he was not a humane man?'

3. 'If you think rightly you will act rightly. It is never honest to have a thought that does not become a part of your experience.'

I do not suppose that this tincture of literary ethics would have remained so clearly in my mind for over thirty years, had it not been disconcertingly obvious that Ezra meant exactly what he said, and had already practised it.

The concrete image, unruffled by an adjective, *was* a thing Ezra would willingly have died for. Rhetoric *was* a thing he would gladly have murdered; and he had already carried out his theory of honest thinking at the expense of considerable financial and perhaps emotional sacrifices. His passionate and austere sincerity acted like a torch upon the young intellectuals of his day. He cast off his home and his country because he was disgusted by its slovenliness of intellectual outlook, although he was certain (with his gifts) of success and reputation had he remained in his own land; and he was wholly unknown and unsupported when he attempted to browbeat London.

Ezra always took any and every risk that came his way in his proclamation of truth, but he sometimes did not take sufficient time to make sure of his truth before he proclaimed it. Yet his courage was a touching and beautiful thing; he landed in Spain at twenty-three years old with five pounds in his pocket and no ostensible means of keeping them there—let alone adding to them. He spent three weeks in Venice, living solely on potatoes (of which there was a momentary glut), so that he could freely nourish his spirit upon its timeless glories. He shook the worth of comfort out of his young contemporaries. This was the third of his dynamic contributions to my own education. He urged me, as he urged all young people under the thrall of domesticity, to fling over our whole background in order to win economic independence from the fruit of our wits.

I am more sure of his literary wisdom to-day than I was at the time. I boggled at his challenge then, partly from sheer cowardice, and partly because the fang of a wrongly construed family affection had struck too deeply into my nervous system; but I knew many others of his pupil-friends who flung themselves with greater courage into the rough surf of the economic struggle and have proved themselves the better swimmers for it. Ezra broke down all pigeon-holes between life and art. He scraped the façade off false morality. Whether he was aware of it or not he believed and preached 'By their fruits ye shall know them' better than many clerics—and with far more purity and passion.

He helped to release any, and every, artist, young or old, whom he came across, from any shackles that prevented the strength of their artistic impulses.

His name will always be sympathetically linked to perhaps the greatest of modern sculptors—Gaudier-Brzeska.

To the poet Yeats (a much older man), Ezra acted as a brilliant knife-grinder. To Joyce he was the tenderest and most skilful of midwives. His were the deftly used instruments that helped to release those strange bantlings, *The Story of an Artist as a Young Man* and *Ulysses*, into the light of day.

The wilderness of London rang with Ezra's voice making straight the way of the Lords.

It is difficult to say how much Ezra Pound did for T. S. Eliot, D. H. Lawrence, or his devoted enemy Wyndham Lewis, but he certainly eased the approach to their goals by helping to prod dangerous stupidities out of their way.

The biology of sex was to the young Ezra a joyous discovery; and he yodelled the necessity of thinking objectivity and the fun of living dangerously, from every house-top in London.

Naturally Ezra was loathed by the morally hide-bound, and despised by orthodox institutions. Scholars he unfortunately outraged, by his inexact but vivid grasp of every subject he discussed. Sometimes he thought that nobody else had discovered what many wiser but more silent artists already knew by heart.

England had already been fortunate in the generation which before the war cleared away the traps and shackles of the late Victorians. Bernard Shaw's rapier had pricked a good deal of stuffing out of the English goose. H. G. Wells had supplied salutary roughage for the intestines of his generation. Galsworthy had started—but alas! not persevered in—stripping the English soul clean of its middle-class snobberies and ferocities. Joseph Conrad had set Polish jewels of thought, with a sailor's courage, into the intricate background of the English language. Henry James was still pursuing earnestly his piercingly intellectual studies on international types of mind, showing up in turn, through his bloodless novels, one by one the qualities and defects of the three countries he best loved and understood: America, England and France.

To Henry James, Ezra Pound gave a continuous loyalty; and one of his most penetrating essays in *Make it New* deals with the tremendous perspicacity of his old and valued friend. Yet, to Ezra, the originality of these great writers seemed already out of date. He was a much younger man than any of the Masters and was perhaps more relentlessly detached in consequence in his outlook upon the modern world.

Ezra flashed upon London like the Angel of the Lord appearing to Ezekiel in the valley of bones, shouting: 'Son of man—stand upon thy feet'. And not until the young man got up and faced the universe with courage, did the Angel Ezra prepare to give him the message, so that the dead bones—breathed upon in the manner suggested by Ezra—might live.

It is perhaps predominantly as a prophet, rather than as a poet, that Ezra benefited his generation; and it is to the fact that so many of his prophecies were on the right lines that he owes his survival as a critic into the present day. Had Jonah been less indigestible how can we be sure that the whale would have expelled him? Yet it was, I think, a tragedy for both parties that the whale of London could not keep down this nimble Jonah who distracted, but so well stimulated, her lethargic stomach. From the moment Ezra left the Anglo-Saxon world he began to suffer more and more from the isolation of his intellectual exile. This wild and wilful child of the Prophets—'a Daniel come to Judgment'—needed the thick padded hide of the antediluvian monster, whose maw he had so precipitately fled from! The most original of men—and Ezra was burning with originality—is partially dependent for his originality upon free and equal companionship; and no companionship can be quite so free as that of those contemporaries who belong to our own race and speak a common tongue.

Ezra had, as a human being, all the failings of a beloved, an only, and a spoilt, child.

He took for granted—without practising—the art of conciliation. He felt that he should be affectionately accepted by all intelligent people, however badly he behaved; and he was *not* so accepted. He thought all his ideas were equally valuable; even when they were little more than irritated yells. He wanted his own way so badly that when he couldn't have it he left the inhospitable shores that refused to give it to him, without giving time for the leaven to act upon the lump.

Ezra must have found very early in life that being a belligerent baby paid. I only met his parents, whom I greatly liked, once. They were a quiet, old-fashioned, and extremely pleasant type of American—common to our early childhood, but less easily discerned now. I can readily believe, however, that his mother may have kept Ezra's red-gold hair in locks; and if she could have induced him to wear Little Lord Fauntleroy suits, I can imagine there is still extant a photograph of the baby Ezra frowning a warning of what he did *not* intend to become, later on.

But being belligerent by itself does not pay poets in the long run. London *had* to listen to William II, but she did not feel obliged to listen to Ezra. The 'noises off' made by the first number of his periodical *Blast* were lost in the thunder of the European War.

Ezra shook the dust of England off his feet, and tried to make his spiritual home across the Channel. France had long been a reservoir for Ezra's mind. Some of the most charming, and perhaps most lasting, of his poems date from the Latin influence. 'Personae' sprang direct from the Troubadours, and 'Riposte' developed the relationship.

Jacopa del Sellaio did not send a message to Ezra through the centuries in vain. 'The eyes of this dead lady', Ezra wrote, 'speak to me,'

For here was love, was not to be drowned out,
And here desire, not to be kissed away,
The eyes of this dead lady speak to me.

An anthology of twentieth-century poetry is poor that does not contain Ezra's 'The Return'.

See, they return; oh, see the tentative
Movements, and the slow feet,
The trouble in the pace and the uncertain
Wavering!
See, they return, one, and by one,
With fear, as half awakened;
As if the snow should hesitate
And murmur in the wind,
And half turn back;
These were the 'Wing'd-with-Awe'
Inviolable.

Gods of the wingèd shoe!
With them the silver hounds,
Snuffing the trace of the air
Haie! Haie!
These were the swift to harry;
These were the keen scented;
These were the souls of blood.
Slow on the leash,
Pallid the leash-men!'

'Plunge', 'A Virginal', 'Pan is Dead' (even Ezra had to write about Pan in those days!)—are not these all poems?

I have read with respect and confusion much of Ezra's later work. Sometimes in the Cantos, I feel again that keen, authentic shiver, I say to myself, 'Whether I understand the sense of this or *not*—it *is* poetry! He wouldn't approve of my saying so, but what happens to the roots of the spine *is* always poetry!' But alas! in Ezra's surcharged 'Cantos' we are taught too much—we shiver too little!

Once Ezra sang—and after singing he left France, and went—more lonely, less companionated still—to Italy; and there he met the only Ruler in the World who noticed him—Mussolini. In an ecstasy, Ezra 'plunged' again, and this time the chronic exile came up with the head of Mussolini firmly grasped between his artist's prehensile fingers—a sorry spectacle!

I came in for a living fragment of this part of Ezra's life. I visited Rapallo—having not seen him for thirty years—and found him with his brave, beautiful, and understanding wife, Dorothy, living above a café, which housed in its front window a bust of the Poet himself. I like to think that it was not the political Ezra—the proud and brittle Fascist—that I really found there; it was something far more endurable. We were looking for a piano, when we came on our first traces of this authentic Ezra. 'Oh,' we were told, 'the Signor Pound is the person to go to—for anything about artists!'

Still many-sided, hard-working and ruthless and yet benevolent, Ezra, besides being a critic, at least something of a scholar, and more than something of a poet, had now brought his penetrating and versatile mind to the study of music—and economics. There in Rapallo he had set to work to release and train—and financially assist—a school of musicians. He had flung himself into music as he flung himself into art—he was still, as he had always been—sea-deep in literature.

Ezra's setting to music of François Villon's ballads was both a literary and musical event. It even reached London on the night of an Election, and rang out upon the B.B.C. But not alone through his own production did Ezra re-vivify the music that came his way. He showed his old spirit of generous comradeship in releasing the music of others. He believed, of course, all kinds of individual things about music, unshared by most musicians. Music must become active, and link up with singing and dancing. The weight and length of each word of a poem must fit the music. But there was something besides music in his exiled heart. Once more he was at work —interpreting, understanding, releasing fellow-creatures. It was the old Ezra whom I found, still eager—still young, still full of stern, redemptive benevolence. He was still at work upon *The Validity of the Object*, and whatever the object was that interested him, Douglas' Social Credit, or musical reconstruction, he set to work immediately to explore and exploit all its active possibilities. No thorns could keep Ezra, without the castle of the Sleeping Beauty, and no Princess within, could he have allowed to sleep on an instant longer than a kiss would take to set her going.

Even as a young man, Ezra had always taken a determined stand on general decencies. It was not licence he wanted; alas! not even freedom—his goal was the forcible enlightenment of mankind. He always sought 'production' rather than profit. He wanted—and I believe still wants—all human beings to have an equal opportunity to prove their worth.

Even as a good Fascist Ezra found it hard to swallow the persecution of the Jews. He got away from the subject when I pounced upon it. The Teutonic mind, he said quickly, was no favourite of his: Mussolini, he implied, did not particularly dislike the Jews.

It is necessary to turn back to Ezra's childhood to find a key to that dire impatience which has led him into so strange a spiritual home as Fascist Italy. It is, alas, the spoiled and wilful child who makes whips and bloodshed take the place of wisdom and social interest!

Nevertheless in Ezra we are dealing with a creative artist who never—however impatient he was—sold his birthright for a mess of pottage. Ezra can be mistaken—more thoroughly mistaken than most people—but he has never been venal. He is one of the few people I have ever met who has never been either inflated or deflated by personal possessions. There is practically no limit to his asceticism for any purpose

—other than asceticism. He lived in 1935 (when I last saw him) in the utmost simplicity, although if he had been a little more conciliatory he could always have earned enough for his comfort—and his wife's; but he never valued anything that money could buy as he valued the integrity of his sharp-shooting mind.

Ezra always grasped the interesting distinction between work—which is all men's heritage and should be their safe delight—and paid employment—which is only a necessity in given conditions and does not imply either security or delight. He accepted Fascism, largely I believe because he mistakenly but honestly thought that Mussolini agreed with him. Mussolini is an Italian, and probably saw that Ezra would be impressed by his economic sympathy. Dictators do not have to make their words come true; but even Dictators may see, at certain periods in their careers, that their words should sound agreeable to important foreigners. Mussolini may well have thought an ardent American poet, with a reputation for moral humanity, exactly the right fish to fry; and so he fried Ezra.

I was never able to grasp the place that either C. H. Douglas or the Italian Führer took in Ezra's mind. He tried hard to impart to me the glow that his partnership with C. H. Douglas in particular threw over his life. (Despairing of my prejudice against Dictators, he soon gave up the attempt to sell me Mussolini.) At least I wholly agreed with him that money—and the mysterious authority it claimed over the modern world—should be debunked as speedily as possible. Duplicity has no place in art; it has no place in morals; it has no place in science; and there seems no particular reason why it should have a place in International Finance. The fact that I was willing to admit some complete overthrow of our financial system—though I never grasped how Douglas could replace it—did something to reconcile Ezra to my continued existence.

We kept off Politics, and came together on Confucius and Chinese poetry. As a man, and as an artist, life has preserved Ezra extraordinarily well. In late middle age he is better-looking than in youth, and obviously exceptionally healthy. He shows nothing, beyond his exaggerated belligerency, of the nervousness of his youth: chairs are quite safe with him. His voice has grown pleasant; and he no longer coughs his way through his arguments. He is still the most vivid and satisfactory of conversationalists. He not only speaks—he hears—and even if he jumps down his visitor's throat the moment he has finished listening, Ezra has first lent him the courtesy of an unrivalled attention.

There may still come a day when both those two ill-conditioned tramps Hitler and Mussolini, have been shaken off the back of a chastened Europe, when Ezra may recover from his political disaster, and his gifts as a critic and a poet shine out once more.

No one could write better than Ezra when he was not trying to score off T. S. Eliot by writing as badly as he knew how; and *how* badly he could write only those who understood how well he might have written, recognize.

Ezra is, alas! a 'happy warrior' with an unhappy career. But not even Mussolini could take from this good comrade his honesty of life, his generosity of heart, his blithe and steadfast wit!

He has been condemned to death as a traitor in War Time but this will not perhaps be so bitter to him as to be condemned to life, after having been proved to be forever in the wrong. Thomas Mann said of Hitler, 'The intellect has touched him and passed him by—he is doomed'. How much more cruelly is this true of Ezra!

If a man becomes, for any reason, a victim to solitary confinement, he loses the great preservative of critical companionship. Ezra needed this 'collective security' more than most people. He needed T. S. Eliot and Conrad Aitken, Paris and London. Straight he always was; and could never, with his fine intellectual integrity, have been anything else; but there is a shade of moral perspicacity which depends upon considering the wills of others as of equal importance to our own, which I feel that even the later Ezra wholly lacked.

He could believe that Force is more necessary than truth—and this is mortal heresy to an artist. Perhaps it is worse than mortal heresy to a man, because it robs him of the free companionship of his brothers—and so drives him into fundamental loneliness. No poet can afford to have the mark of Cain upon his brow—it is too isolating.

6

MARGARET MACDONALD BOTTOME

It would not be true of my grandmother to say that she was a saint, but she was the most enthralling—thrilled, and thrilling—Christian it has ever been my lot to meet.

Whether her extraordinary courage and optimism were caused by her faith in God, or whether her faith in God was caused by her extraordinary optimism, I have never felt able to decide. Both were equally there, and carried her as buoyantly forward, as the waves lift a gull, through all the stormy vicissitudes of her eventful life.

Poverty, hard work, the hammer blows of grief—she bore them all with a gay, unshaken fortitude. She did not know what the word 'resignation' meant. She blazed her way through every obstacle and trial with triumphant strength.

'Life is like a tunnel,' she once wrote to me, when I was threatened with consumption, 'you may feel quite sure that when it is darkest you are drawing near the other end—there *will* be light.'

Margaret MacDonald was the second of eighteen children, nine of which lived to maturity. Her father died when her mother was only forty-five, leaving his large family practically penniless. His heroic widow and her no less heroic eldest daughter managed somehow or other to keep all their wolves at bay. Margaret was always used to hard work and could successfully tackle any kind of domestic problem.

I remember her darns as masterpieces of creative art; you literally could not tell a mended from an unmended part of a garment. I have good reason to be grateful for this particular talent. I frequently tore my clothes as a child, and on one occasion was threatened with some severe penalty if I sinned again. I had on a beautiful white muslin frock, and suddenly summoned by some ecstatic vision of childhood flung myself over a fence to reach my goal. A nail tore a huge three-cornered piece out of the very front of my Sunday garment. In an agony I sought the Irish cook, who was my special crony, and told her the fate that lay before me. 'Never you mind, Phyll*us*,' she remarked. 'Youse come wid me to your grandmother!' Secretly we reached my grandmother's room and found her rocking peacefully in her chair by the window. She entered instantly into the conspiracy, and I appeared at dinner in an immaculate frock, invisibly mended, ironed, and triumphant. Neither my conscience nor my grandmother's as much as turned a hair.

I think my grandmother never greatly cared for domesticity, she merely took it in her cheerful stride. She paid for it to be done for her if she had the money; and did it for herself if she hadn't.

I only remember two stories of her early youth, but both were characteristic of her. She was fond of writing letters, and could not afford sufficient stamps. She prayed earnestly for them one night—and sure enough there they were—in a letter on her plate next morning. It had occurred to a distant and richer friend that Margaret might be short of stamps.

When she was seventeen she had a severe toothache. 'I am never going to stand this pain again', Margaret said firmly to her family. She walked to the nearest dentist, whom she terrorized into taking out every tooth in her head—all good except the one that happened to be aching—and then walked back, suffering but undaunted.

She married early in life a pioneer Englishman, who had come to the American Continent at the age of twenty-four, because the Vicar of his parish in Derbyshire did not allow him to take prayer meetings in the same village.

My grandfather, Francis Bottome, was a gentle, delicate, rather didactic poet-minister. He wrote one extremely good hymn—still sung, I believe, in both Episcopal and Methodist churches in the United States. He came to Canada as a circuit rider in the Wesleyan Church, and for years ministered to the Blackfeet Indians. He was then sent to Brooklyn in the U.S.A. as a helper to the pastor of the Sands Street Church. There he met Margaret MacDonald and her family, and subsequently joined the Methodist Church and married Margaret. He was a precise, accurate and orderly person, beloved and respected by all who knew him.

Margaret bore him four sons and one girl child, equally treasured by both, who died at five years old.

For many years after her marriage my grandmother passed into a sort of eclipse; and I have been told nothing of this stage of her career, though we had a photograph of her, taken when she was twenty-eight, a sad, handsome, rather haunting photograph. 'She never looked like that to me,' my father used to say of it, 'she was always smiling.'

Had Margaret Bottome lived to-day I think she would have been as world famous a character as Madame Chiang Kai-Shek, Eleanor Roosevelt or Dorothy Thompson. But she lived in an era when women did not become great; and were not publicly known except in a very limited sense. You could be a good woman or a bad woman—and that was about all.

My grandmother was a good one; and that her private life did break its bonds and force her out into a large measure of publicity was entirely due to a financial misfortune.

Until she was over forty Margaret was the silent, suppressed, very efficient wife of a Methodist pastor, sent every two years to a new pastorate—sometimes in the country and sometimes in a town—never having a permanent home or a 'continuing city'.

The shock that brought her out of this never very natural situation was that a highly-thought of Deacon or Elder absconded overnight with every penny my grandfather possessed. My grandfather, a most cautious and saving person, had thought it a mere matter of form to act as his deacon's guarantor over the week-end; and he now found himself worse than penniless. He not only had nothing, but he had guaranteed what amounted to a considerable portion of his future earnings over the next few years. He might have been excused this final overthrow; but his stern sense of duty persuaded him to pay back the last farthing of this infamous transaction.

My grandmother at once stepped into the gap. They were at the time stationed in Tarrytown, New York, where many well-to-do people lived on their country estates. Some of them were already known to my grandmother; and she began to give undenominational talks of a religious nature to a group of them, which were highly appreciated. She decided to continue these 'talks' on a larger scale, and to accept payment for them.

Almost immediately Margaret found herself stepping into a life of the widest publicity her time could afford.

I have heard many first-rate speakers in my lifetime, religious and otherwise, but I do not believe anyone—including Hitler—had gifts like my grandmother's for oratory; or her invariable and instantaneous grip upon her audiences.

She had an enormous, effortless, carrying voice, full of music. She had no nervousness whatever; and an admirable humour prevented her dramatic powers from overwhelming gravity; and she always spoke with complete sincerity and common sense.

She was not a great thinker, and though she read constantly and remembered what she read, she confined her reading mainly to religious subjects. 'All my theology is Jesus', she used to say. She knew her Bible inside out. Lit by constant prayer and meditation, the lessons of Christianity illustrated by anecdotes from her own life or the lives of others, sounded so true, so new, so startling, that her audiences never tired of listening to her. Time stood still while the spell she wove stole over them; and when she had finished, it was always too soon for her enraptured audiences.

I don't know how Margaret guessed that she had this power, but with her voice and with her pen—like the maiden in Wordsworth's poem—she could 'haunt, and startle, and waylay'. And no doubt—as the maiden may have felt—she had not got this power for nothing. She was without the slightest technical training either as a writer or a speaker; and she had been notoriously silent for many years; but as she herself might have quoted 'Out of the fullness of the heart the mouth speaketh'. Certainly her heart had long been full; and she knew without hesitation what it had been filled with.

Bok, that genius among journalists, was the first to realize what—as Hollywood might describe it—'a natural' he might win for his *Ladies' Home Journal* in Margaret, if he could be the first to secure the exclusive use of her pen. She undertook to write for him a series of 'Heart to heart talks', a phrase coined by herself which later passed into American slang. It was a series that lasted for over a quarter of a century.

Margaret had already founded a new society, 'The King's Daughters'; and the *Ladies' Home Journal* both widened the Society's sphere and added a religious lustre, as well as a wider public, to their own famous magazine. The King's Daughters Society was equally open to Catholics or to members of any of the Free Churches. No dogma tinged any of its tenets. It was based entirely upon 'The Sermon upon the Mount'. The King's Daughters undertook to act upon these utterances. 'I was an hungered and ye gave me meat; thirsty and ye gave me drink; a stranger and ye took me in; naked and ye clothed me; sick and ye visited me; in prison and ye came unto me'. They wore for badge a flat silver Maltese cross, fastened by a small purple ribbon, inscribed with the letters, 'I.H.N.', standing for 'In His Name'.

At first the 'Daughters' formed circles of ten, with a yearly-elected President, but later this was changed to wider circles with indeterminate numbers, At my grandmother's death the organization numbered over 300,000 members. Although numerically considerably less at the present time, it still flourishes, especially in the South and West. Whenever my grandmother spoke, and she spoke whenever she was 'called' to go and speak, these circles sprang up about her path. Their power for good was enormous, for they were not limited by anything but an individual application of the Beatitudes.

My grandmother once having founded this society left its organization in the hands of others. She inspired it—she remained its lifelong President. She wrote for its magazine—but she knew herself better than to tie herself down to the Letter of the Law. The spirit was her business.

It was astonishing to everyone who knew her how little her increasing public life interfered with my grandmother's private relationships. It is unfortunately unusual to find that a deeply religious person is at his or her best in their private lives. But of my grandmother, in spite of her impetuous nature, it could truthfully be said that her greatest successes were her nearest relationships.

Everywhere she went she made and kept new and dear friends; but her four sons and her husband, remained the dearest and most devoted of her companion-lovers.

Her brothers and sisters clung to her all through her life, and always came first to her, in any emergency, for counsel or generosity.

My grandfather never quite succeeded in taming her—and sometimes, rather too often perhaps, tried to repress her dynamic energies—but he loved her and took her advance into a world that had never been his, with unflinching humility.

We—her first and I think most beloved grandchildren—were born at a date when my grandmother was already a public character, so that we never knew her as her sons knew her, in private life.

She thundered through our lives at dramatic intervals like an express train through a silent landscape. She left us gaping—but as she thundered past she noticed us; and made no mistakes as to what kind of grandchildren she had—or how to deal with them.

It is curious to read her letters to my other (English) grandmother—a dull, rich, rather narrow-mindedly religious woman.

The grandmothers had been friends before my father fell in love with Rachel Leatham's daughter, on a visit with her mother to America, made in order to meet my grandmother Bottome.

The letters go on steadily through the years, my English

grandmother had Margaret's letters typed from 1880 on; and a friend of hers sent them to me long after both grandmothers were dead.

They were almost entirely about religion and—us! But to this day the spirit of my grandmother springs out of the old pages with all her dynamic, incredible liveliness, as if they were the voice of to-morrow, rather than of a faraway yesterday. Her religion was as natural to her as bread; and bread—by which she would have meant all her natural relationships—as sacred to her as her religion. I suppose she had no style, but nobody else but Margaret Bottome ever wrote as she wrote or spoke as she spoke. What she had was a voice—an emanation of a ceaselessly active, ceaselessly loving and generous personality. It was impossible not to think of her as a genius—a genius even of the first water—and the work of art she produced was her own character.

Of the three main interests of human beings—sex, money, and religion—my grandmother was only interested in the last.

It is presumable that she had some sex life, since she produced five children; but not I think of a very conscious kind.

I never remember hearing her mention the subject of sex, however remotely, and as she was a great talker, and never refrained from saying anything she wanted to say before any of us, I presume that had she been interested in the subject we should have heard of it.

I am sure she loved my grandfather in a tender and deeply attached manner.

Children she accepted as a gift from the Lord, and all of hers received from her a stream, in fact a torrent, of generous love and encouragement, as well as the example of her splendid courage.

The worst griefs of her life were the loss of her girl child, and of her grown son—a man of brilliant promise—at the early age of thirty-three; but neither of these tragedies was ever allowed to darken the joy of others, or to change her own fundamental trust in Life. Her 'joy' *was* 'in the Lord', and that is where her lost ones were—with It. It was in fact she who was for a little while lost—not they. I have never known anyone who took death—her own or that of those she loved —with such an unruffled serenity. She appeared to believe—and obviously from her behaviour *did* believe—that death was a triumphant step into a radiant eternity.

Money, the second great human incentive, Margaret quite simply ignored. She didn't dislike money, she wasn't ashamed of it, or of the lack of it—when she had it she spent it generously on gifts for others.

The only acid remark to be found in her whole correspondence is upon a sermon of my grandfather's. 'Mr. Bottome', she wrote to her sister-friend Rachel, 'gave us a very fine sermon this morning upon casting all our care upon the Lord. The text he took was "Consider the lilies how they grow—they toil not, neither do they spin". It would be well sometimes if Mr. Bottome took his text a little more practically to heart.'

Margaret herself literally cast *all* her care upon the Lord, and went her way without it; but unlike some people who act upon this principle, to the dismay of their friends and relatives, Margaret, while casting her care away, fulfilled all the duties of a bread-winner.

Her earnings contributed largely to the upkeep of her home; and helped to start her youngest son in life. She managed to fulfil all her duties as a mother in spite of her public life; a fact that was proved by the success her four sons made of their careers. Hers was a greatness that inspired but never shadowed the children she had brought into the world. Her two eldest sons became well-known preachers in the Episcopal Church; the eldest was a brilliant orator; the second was more of an essayist and poet; both were singularly beloved and gifted men. Her third son, a very promising young physician, died at the age of thirty-three; her youngest son became a lawyer, and devoted his keen and logical wits to the New York Life Insurance Society, for whom in later life he acted as legal counsellor and governor until his retirement.

My grandmother had a peculiarly strengthening and inspiring effect upon her intimates. She gave them all the strength of a deep, possessive love without its tyranny. Her loved ones were free to work, to love, to play—with or without her. Whatever in their choice she *could approve* received her full support. She praised whatever she admired without criticism, envy or jealousy. What she neither approved nor understood she left alone, unless she thought it was actual 'sin', when she said so in no uncertain voice and left it at that. She treated her grandchildren as she treated her children, only she saw less of us, as the ocean generally rolled between. My eldest sister, Wilmett, always called her 'my girl grandmother', and talked to her as to a contemporary. She was more famous when it came to my turn to understand her, and awe mingled with my love. 'Be happy—and you'll be good!' she once mysteriously remarked to me when I was six years old. A treasured remark, which might well be used by all those who study child psychology. An equally quickening remark of hers lingers in my memory. We were suffering from the visit of a strange aunt, returning from her honeymoon with a beloved uncle. Both grandparents were staying with us. While sitting on the piazza a mosquito lit upon the bridge of my Uncle George's handsome Roman nose; without an instant's hesitation I slapped it dead, rather startling my uncle in the process. His newly-made wife flew into a passionate temper and rated me soundly for my irreverence. To my horror both grandparents, hitherto my staunchest supporters, added their reproofs to hers. As soon as she and my uncle had taken their departure I flung myself upon my grandparents. 'There really *was* a mosquito,' I told them, 'and I had to kill it before it stung Uncle George!' My grandmother gave me a penetrating man-to-man glance as she replied: '*We* know it was a mosquito, child, and we know *why* you did it—but to your Aunt Annie, it was *not* a mosquito!' This was the first time that it had occurred to me that there might be different views taken of the same fact. I needed no further explanation, and my grandmother gave me none. She always knew exactly where to stop.

I always thought of her as my 'rich grandmother', and the English one, who lived in Grosvenor Square, as my 'poor' one. We had every reason as children to suppose our American grandmother rich, for to our English vicarage, punctual as the beats of a heart, came several weeks or days before Christmas —dependent on the then far more uncertain Atlantic—a marvellous wooden packing case. Inside this case were the treasures of Eldorado. Everything a child could fancy—toys, garments of an exotic splendour—each child's taste divined or imagined with a perfect felicity. I never remember one shadow of a disappointment over these carefully chosen gifts. Marvellous boxes of American 'candy' were shared by the entire household; and each parcel done up by my grandmother herself was a poem. The coloured paper matched, the ribbon matched, there was a name on a brilliant Christmas card. Long before we ever knew her, she had made herself a formidable reputation to live up to in her grandchildren's minds; but when we met her, she lived up to it.

When we went to America to live, I saw with astonishment how small her home was and cried, 'But, Grandmother, I always thought you were so rich—not like poor Grannie Fowler!'

My grandmother shook with laughter. 'Well,' she said, 'so I *am* rich! You were perfectly right—but I often don't know where the money's to come from!'

Margaret was like Emerson who, when told by a Seventh Day Adventist that the end of the world was upon them, merely replied: 'Well, I can get on quite well without it!'

Once when my grandmother was earning more money than ever before, she overdrew her bank balance. Having been informed by telephone of this unpleasant fact she sent the maid with a cheque to the grocer; and sent the cash to the bank, a transaction hurriedly put right by her doctor son on his return from his rounds.

Perhaps one of the secrets of my grandmother's tingling vitality was her humour. She was sometimes sick, but never sorry. She could laugh at anything—including herself.

She often quoted with fond appreciation her beloved friend, Hannah Smith's equally fond criticism of her: 'Thee has wings, Margaret, but thee flops!'

My grandmother sometimes 'flopped' when her indomitable will was crossed, and sometimes she let her emotions sweep her away from her common sense. My father used to quote one occasion when she had been invited as a speaker to attend a great meeting at the Carnegie Hall on the Armenian atrocities. Many other speakers spoke first, each taking the line of pious horror and indignation against the Turks. My grandmother slept throughout several of those somewhat verbose denunciations. When it was her turn to be introduced by the Chairman, she electrified the whole hall by a passionate tribute to the American flag, denouncing its degradation and rousing every member of her large audience to a sense of personal responsibility for the suffering Armenians. It was characteristic of her to swerve from what would have seemed to her a useless judgment of others into herself accepting an active responsibility for a wrong done.

I think she never saw an evil she did not immediately feel it was her business to solve. Long before the faulty nations of this small earth realized it, Margaret Bottome knew with a burning certainty that 'we are all members one of another'.

Nothing roused her wrath as greatly as when a religious form obscured or falsified the spirit of religion itself.

She could be terrible when roused; as ruthless as an artist at the sight of a faked work of art.

Once a very famous and fascinating English clergyman was caught by my grandmother in the act of kissing a 'fallen woman' whom he had set out to reclaim. 'Your mother', he told my father, who was a friend of his, 'simply broke me to pieces—it was worse than anything I can imagine at the Day of Judgment!'

But if my grandmother 'broke him to pieces' it is only fair to say that, years later, when she thought him wholly reformed, she picked up the pieces and put them together again, introducing him as the saint she thought him, to all her American scene.

Margaret was as a rule uncritically merciful in her judgment of people. 'All my mother's servants are angels', as one

occasion, caught hold of her to exclaim, 'don't you remember who I am?'

My grandmother paused and replied: 'Is there any particular reason why I should?'

Although she lived in a sentimental period of American life, my grandmother was not—*au fond*—a sentimentalist. She *was* highly emotional; but when she had an emotion she did something about it.

She was always actively 'on her Father's business', and nobody else's interested her: not even her own.

Outwardly she was the most gay and cheerful person imaginable, but one of her sons has told me that sometimes when he returned at night he could hear her groaning in prayer to God about her sins; but she never groaned about anyone else's—even to God.

My father, who was ten years the eldest of her family, was for many years her chief companion-child; and it is from him, and her weekly letters to him when he lived in England, that I know most about my grandmother.

They wrote to each other with the utmost intimacy, and yet my mother, who was a highly critical and somewhat jealous lover, never resented these letters which she always shared. Indeed, she had—as the other daughters-in-law had—a strong personal devotion to her most unexacting mother-in-law.

My grandmother believed the marriage between my father and mother to be 'perfect' and she was, I think, largely responsible for keeping it at a higher level of happiness than it would have kept without her. None of her sons' marriages were perhaps quite as ideal as Margaret thought them; but perhaps she did not think them quite as ideal as she let them believe she thought them.

It was only her sons—never her daughters-in-law—that she ever took to task for their failings. Their love could stand her 'precious balms', and they were equally free to tell their mother of her own failings.

'Be still, Mother,' her fastidious and cautious second son once demanded on a public occasion when he feared an outbreak. 'George,' she replied with her irrepressible chuckle, 'I'll be still—when I'm dead!'

I suppose, from my father's description, that my grandfather, though dearly loved by my grandmother, may sometimes have appeared to her in the light of a 'cross'. As a grandfather he was impeccable; rosy cheeked, with eyes as blue as a speedwell in a hedge; tranquil; benevolent; and the most tireless and wise of playfellows; but to my father as a child he was almost cruelly stern. As a young man he had believed in unspoiling the child by the rod; and had particularly felt that his eldest son was in need of this brisk penalty.

We should say now that he was probably jealous of the absorbing love my grandmother gave her first-born, but at the time any punishment he inflicted no doubt appeared to my grandfather as a duty. He was a scholar; precise, accurate, and full of spiritual integrity.

I cannot think that my grandmother even in her most submissively domestic days was ever either precise or accurate; and her integrity, though just as real as my grandfather's, was of a flashing, rather than a systematic, order.

For many years my grandfather was extremely delicate, and his health was one of my grandmother's special cares. She herself had a magnificent constitution which she overworked with general impunity, and only occasional short physical protests, until she was over seventy, when she was successfully operated on for cancer. The doctor who operated on her told her that a recurrence would be unlikely if she could dismiss all thought of the illness. She did it in the following way.

All the nurses at the hospital adored her, and when she was about to leave she called them all to her room, embraced them as daughters with the utmost warmth and gratitude, and told them, to their astonished dismay, that she was never going to see any of them again. The hospital and all that was in it she must put out of her life for ever.

Within two months she resumed her Drawing Room Talks, and within a year she was speaking to audiences of over a thousand people. During this year she attended a religious conference where she spoke three times a day to large audiences, and talked all the time between.

Rather naturally she lost her voice and had to send for a doctor. 'Mrs. Bottome,' the doctor told her, 'you simply *must* be quiet for a bit and not use your voice *at all*!' 'I will be quiet, doctor. I *will*!' my grandmother whispered—and for twelve hours she never spoke and remained in bed. Then she caught a train for Nashville, Tennessee, which was a day and a night journey, and spoke the following day to separate audiences of white and coloured people.

During the last few years of her life my grandmother was more than ever active, travelling constantly from city to city, pouring out her heart to her great audiences as if she knew that her time was short and dared not waste one drop of the great love she felt for—and inspired in—mankind.

The invasion of her public career had never had a harmful or limiting effect upon her personality, or her more intimate ties. Among her personal friends, and they were numberless, I have only heard of one that had an adverse effect upon her deep and tranquil heart. There was in her inner circle of friends a dangerous hysteric whose devotion to my grandmother, especially in later life, was a sore trial to all her friends and relations. While my grandmother lived, the harm done by this depressing satellite was neutralized by my grandmother's influence over her; but there is no doubt that Margaret suffered both in her work and in her daily life from this much younger friend, who, nevertheless, gave her a great deal of practical assistance in the constant public calls upon her, while sometimes blinding her keen insight by perpetual flattery—used for that purpose. Margaret knew that there was much to forgive in this 'daughter-friend', but it never occurred to her that you could, or should, 'give up' a person you forgave. She always used imperfect instruments with undimmed generosity; never expecting as much of others as she ruthlessly expected of herself. She gave her last talk in Albany to 1,500 people, against her doctor's orders, without apparent ill effects, three days before she died.

Death came to her swiftly and easily as the Friend she had always believed him. She had a slight cold and falling asleep, a cerebral haemorrhage took place; and she never woke again.

She was, when she died, as she wrote on her seventy-ninth birthday a few weeks earlier, 'seventy-nine years young'.

It is said that America has a short memory for its public favourites, but in my grandmother's case I have not found this a true criticism.

As a novelist I have often lectured from city to city all over the United States, and I have never yet addressed a single audience out of which some individual has not come to me afterwards and said: 'I knew your grandmother!' or, 'My mother has never forgotten hearing Margaret Bottome speak'.

Once Mrs. James Roosevelt took me to see a very old and, as she told me, very hard-hearted and worldly old lady, who was to give a great luncheon party in a house more like a world-famous museum than a home, it was so full of priceless treasures. When Mrs. Roosevelt introduced me to this hard and worldly old woman a miracle took place. Age, and the mask of her worldliness, fell from her. She looked suddenly young. She caught both my hands: 'You're my Margaret's granddaughter,' she said, her eyes full of tears, 'I *know* you belong to Margaret—you have her eyes!'

She seemed suddenly to have picked up some lost and happy secret. Then her butler approached her with the announcement of special visitors, and the mask slipped again over her features.

She was once more a cold and dominating old woman about to give a luncheon to her brittle world.

'Well, that's the first time I ever knew she even *had* a heart,' Mrs. Roosevelt murmured to me as we left the house.

The only outward and permanent mark of my grandmother's long service to her country is one that she would I think have most appreciated.

In the heart of the proud, race-conscious South—Norfolk, Virginia—there is a hospital called The Margaret Bottome

Memorial Hospital, run on funds collected yearly by the King's Daughters Society, for white and coloured babies together.

Everything in this hospital is for both races equally. The nurses and doctors are both white and coloured, and serve white or coloured babies with the same care.

When you pass that door, under that little cross, all human beings are members together of the same Family. I think my grandmother must have been the first of the Universalists. For her there was only One God, the Father of us all, and in this Faith she lived; and moved; and had her being.

7

'HEROINE UP TO DATE: VICTORIA DRUMMOND'

Victoria Drummond, the only surviving God-daughter of Queen Victoria, belongs by natural right to the heroines of English history.

In the late fourteen-hundreds, James the Fourth of Scotland was passionately in love with Margaret Drummond, one of the three beautiful sisters of the House of Concraig, from which House Victoria's family, the Drummonds of Megginch, are directly descended.

There is strong evidence that James and Margaret were secretly married, and indeed such a marriage could be the only valid reason for the drastic act taken by the authorities, who saw no better way of obtaining a more ambitious marriage for Scotland than by murdering Margaret. They went so far as to poison the three beautiful sisters together, at Mass, in the Cathedral of Dunblane through the medium of the Sacramental Wine; and there they lie to this day, beneath the stone upon which they knelt to take their death from the altar.

One interesting point in this story is that in order to get rid of Margaret's influence all three sisters had to be murdered. Three sisters of equal devotion to each other are indeed an enduring feature of the Drummond family, and in this generation our heroine Victoria is the second of such a three. Three more are blossoming to meet the next turn of the tide; and any man or woman making an enemy of any one of three Drummond sisters is always liable to find himself in the same predicament as the royal marriage makers in 1480. It would be safer for him to get rid of them all three simultaneously; and finally.

It is a comfort to know that the bereaved family still had two earlier kings to their credit, since Robert III married Arabella Drummond in the early fourteenth century and their son James I of Scotland was the 'poet-king' to whom Queen Victoria was well aware that she owed, through Arabella, her Stuart descent.

Nor was James the Fourth wholly unfaithful to his murdered Margaret. There is a small and very fine portrait of him holding in his hand a Marguerite daisy, taken, tradition tells us, well after his subsequent marriage.

It may be the blood of kings or it may be some less ascertainable fluid that is to be found in the veins of the present Drummond sisters. But there is something about them which it is difficult to match. The eldest of them has a delicate something in her carriage which hints of immovable decisions. Victoria might seem merely taller than the other two; the youngest has very clear and brilliant green eyes. Their manners are friendly but deprecating, rather timid than otherwise, and yet behind their superficial gentleness is an iron security of will, that it would be dangerous to knock against.

None of them is ever to be found in the middle of a room; or doing anything to attract the attention of others.

In spite of the fact that their courtesy is of an old-fashioned and ceremonious type, they are extremely up-to-date in their mental honesty; and invariably practise what they believe.

The eldest runs a club in Lambeth in which many overworked, middle-aged women have been trained into gay acrobats, while not without further development of a moral nature.

Victoria, after early and adventurous travels with her father, took up engineering and became with great credit an engineer in the Mercantile Marine. She had had a passion for engines from her earliest childhood, and she passed from her sea service as an acknowledged expert, into a big Engineering Firm; and was sent as their representative agent to all the great International Exhibitions of Engineering, in San Francisco, Leipsig, and Vienna.

Had the Royal Navy been open to women, it is no doubt upon one of His Majesty's ships that Victoria would have functioned during the war. Nor was she without qualifications for the Royal Navy. She was a good boxer and as a Junior Engineer she knocked out a Chinese Bandit with whom she found herself at odds, thereby saving the expedition she was on from disaster. Victoria who was on the Reserve of the Mercantile Marine returned to sea directly war was declared.

Outside the U.S.S.R. only one other woman, a Swede, shares the career of ship's engineer with Victoria. It would be safe to say that no other woman has been so continuously on convoy since the war began. 'Miss Second' has sailed on every sea; in all conceivable weathers, exposed to every possible danger from above or below. Almost always the only woman on her ship; always the only woman in her crew, she has faced in imperturbable loneliness, hourly risks of death and disaster.

Volumes would be needed to tell of her escapes and adventures from submarine and dive-bomber, but the seal of the Silent Service is as safe with Victoria as if she were the rock of Gibraltar by which she has so often sailed. With an appearance of complete candour those smiling serene grey eyes could fool the most experienced of snoopers. Knowing exactly what it is her duty to hide—she hides it—and hides no more than is necessary; so that it appears as if she hid nothing.

In the same way she uses her matchless courage, unobtrusively and in the exact quantity needed for the emergency. There has never been occasion in all these death-driven, adventurous years in which Victoria has not had enough courage; but no Drummond ever splutters with their qualities. They retire from everything but danger.

Perhaps the hardest of all Victoria's war experiences was to hear that her two sisters in Lambeth had been buried under a wall of concrete while on duty as air-raid wardens, though miraculously rescued; and then bombed not once but three times out of successive homes. On each occasion they went back to the same spot, as if nothing had happened except some small mis-adventure to a bathroom tap. During those worst war years the sisters could not hear what had happened to Victoria. She might lie under the weight of any sea; nor could she hear for weeks or months whether the bones of her sisters might not be scattered with the stones of London. One thing they all three knew, that their spirits would be as undivided in death, as those of David and Jonathan, or those three quiet beauties beneath the aisle in the Cathedral of Dunblane.

During those last years between wars, Victoria and her youngest sister travelled all over Europe, especially in Germany. Victoria travelled unostentatiously for her firm, her sister for a firm of London decorators. But Victoria was a highly skilled engineer; and both were first-rate photographers.

There could be no harm, they felt, in taking photographs of Diesel engines in full flight, or any other special kind of interesting subject—that those skilled and innocent eyes might feel to be of eventual use to their small menaced Island.

They talked foreign languages with ease and correctness, and always made friends with their fellow travellers. Often in pre-war Germany after the rise of Hitler, they were told behind shuttered windows, in breathless whispers, horrible first-hand accounts of Nazi cruelties. They travelled cheaply, foot-free and inconspicuous with only the luggage that they could carry. No more harmless and care-free holiday women ever travelled through one Nazi-shaken, menaced country to another. On March 11th 1938 they reached Vienna simultaneously with the German army of occupation, to be implored by an agitated Embassy official either to wear a Union Jack or keep an arm in a sling since otherwise they would be forced to give the Hitler salute.

'Oh, no, I don't think we should do that!' Victoria replied with a faint reflective smile in her eyes.

On reaching their hotel they were immediately locked into their bedroom and ordered not to go near the window as Hitler was about to pass in a victory procession through the street on which their hotel faced. As soon as they were alone they slid cautiously to the window and took photographs of Hitler perched aloft, surrounded and covered by his guards, in his specially armoured car.

When they were allowed to descend into the hall, they were pointed out to a German officer as the English women who had just entered Vienna aggravatingly unaware of the day's event. This seems to have infuriated the German officer for with true Prussian politeness, he hurried across the hall, and stamped on Victoria's foot. He had made an unfortunate selection for Victoria, with one swift gesture, sent the young man spinning across the floor, to crash into the nearest wall with such force that he fell to the ground in a heap. Picking himself up, this remarkable specimen of German manhood clicked his heels together, and bowed profoundly. This act of spiritual submission surprised Victoria almost more than her physical competence had surprised him.

The next day, as inconspicuously as they had entered it, the Drummond sisters departed from Vienna. On their journey home they shared a carriage with agonized refugees, who soon confided to the sisters that they expected to be turned back to almost certain death as soon as the Passport Officer came to examine their passports. Soon after this the Passport Officer entered their carriage. The train was standing in the station about to depart, when a very surprising accident took place; somehow or other the deeply apologetic Victoria knocked the Passport Officer's hat off through the open window onto the platform. Springing from the carriage in his agitation, he inadvertently left his stamp and various papers behind him on the seat of the carriage.

Victoria had all the refugees' passports carefully and expertly stamped by the time he returned. Both she and her sister were so full of explanations and apologies as well as of innumerable questions about their own passports, that he never discovered what had taken place. Neither sister batted an eyelid while carrying out this impromptu performance; and they managed to return to their small and inconspicuous Island with all their photographs and the two cameras intact.

When war broke out, each sister immediately took the job best suited for her.

They had a house, now long ago in ashes, of quite extraordinary charm opening onto a slum thoroughfare. A bright yellow door led into a sort of fairyland. Carpets and painted screens from China, scarlet cooking pots from Holland, pictures and precious objects from all over the world, greeted the astonished eyes.

The sisters kept no maid. They took their chief meal of the day near their work, and looked after the house for themselves. In spite of London smuts, everything in it shone with the special cleanness of an art.

If you were invited to a meal by the Drummond sisters, before the war made meals cheerless and choiceless, it was already prepared for you, so that your hostesses seemed without urgency or pre-occupation. If it was in summer time, the entertainment was laid in the garden. For somehow or other they had made a garden—a whole miniature landscape—like a Chinese garden, out of what had been a back yard—including a pool for goldfish, with a lotus—or perhaps it was only a water lily—presiding over the scene. I remember sharing one such meal in the summer before the war, with a benign and pleasant Bishop. We supped on cold salmon, with a salad a French chef might have been proud to achieve, followed by bowls of strawberries and cream, to the cheerful accompaniment of sparkling cider. The ease with which this beautiful meal appeared—the art with which all traces of it vanished—remain forever a Drummond mystery.

The three sisters were what even people with unambitious incomes would describe as 'poor'. But there were no more signs of poverty about them than there would have been of riches, had they been rich. They lived as they could afford to live, choosing whatever they valued most; and cheerfully renouncing all that they valued less.

The Lambeth district in which they lived close to the river was a magnet for bombs. I do not know if the two sisters were nearly killed as often as Victoria; but they were nearly killed quite often enough.

Victoria's adventures cannot yet be told. The only one chosen by the authorities for publicity, was that of a dive bomber attack, on an old and slow-moving ship crossing a wintry sea. There seemed no chance at all for Victoria's ship. The bomber was right overhead and had singled her out for its load. An officer, looking down into the engine room, saw 'Miss Second' carrying on alone, having sent the engine-room crew on deck. Hot oil was pouring over her face from a leaking pipe, while she held up a vital part of the machinery with one arm, and pushed her little ship on its way at twelve knots, its normal speed being eight; and by this expert handling the little ship zig-zagged its way into safety.

Victoria had not thought this an unusually severe adventure, so that she was surprised when her ship arrived in port to be given an extra two days' leave ashore in order to appear before the King to receive an M.B.E.

No doubt she was glad of the extra days and nights, though as she elected to remain with her sisters, it is problematical whether they were quiet nights. At least she had the satisfaction of having helped to persuade their intrepid mother to retire to the country, where, though still in reach of bombs, she was outside a target area.

On one of her later convoys, Norfolk, Virginia, discovered and welcomed Victoria. Perhaps, since it is itself a city of ships and ship-builders, with no mean history, Norfolk Virginia felt a special affinity with this sea-daughter of Britain. At any rate this American city gave to Victoria a most signal and generous recognition. A Restaurant was presented to Lambeth, in her honour called after her name, with sufficient funds to last as a feeding centre throughout the war. It was a disappointment on the visit of Eleanor Roosevelt to this country that a meeting could not have been arranged between these two remarkable women, in whom it is possible to sense a strong spiritual resemblance. During the short visit which the President's wife paid to Great Britain, in one of the dark hours of her long struggle, Victoria was just off on a particularly cold and cruel North Sea convoy. Her one desire was to meet Eleanor Roosevelt. But the visit, like a flash of strong and kindly light illuminating many hearts that will never forget her, was too brief for their meeting to be arranged and Victoria went back to the sea without the hail of that fellow traveller—always willing as she herself was willing, to face unknown seas.

Upon one occasion, an official from the British Admiralty rather superciliously questioned Victoria. 'What steps would you take, Miss Drummond,' he demanded, 'should your ship be attacked by a dive bomber?' 'The engine room steps, sir,' Victoria replied demurely, with a glint in her grey eyes.

It would be difficult to estimate or even understand the trust and loyalty Victoria rouses in her engine room, unless you were one of her crew; because no one else has seen Victoria in constant action. They have; and they know her for what she is. For five years, she has been chosen by the authorities, always for the hardest tasks, without any more leave than her rank and service warrant.

The danger, the hard conditions, have sometimes been too much for one of the crew but never for 'Miss Second'. On one terrible voyage a stoker, gone temporarily out of his mind, attacked a fellow stoker in the engine room and would have murdered him had Victoria not stepped between them, saying, 'You know you are not allowed to play games in here!' The stoker dropped the iron bar with which he was about to brain his fellow, shocked into common sense, and returned to his job.

I doubt if any man ever offended Victoria twice. There is about her so calm and cheerful a dignity, such suave courtesy mixed with such iron resolution, that the wish to offend would be unlikely to arise. Most men would simply know better than to try.

Humour and kindliness, combined with the knowledge of her own business, and no desire to interfere with the business of others, make a good armour for a woman in a crew composed of men. They are indeed a good armour for any human being in all the adventures of life; and no one ever kept this armour so entire or so bright—as Victoria Drummond.